CW00727506

This Journal Belongs to:

....

Instagram
@limitlessabundance_official

info@limitlessabundanceofficial.com

@limitlessabundance

Copyright @ 2021 Limitless Abundance

All rights reserved.

No parts of this publication may be reproduced, distributed, or transmitted in any form, or by any means, including photocopying, recording or other electronic or mechanical methods, without prior written permission from the publisher.

Law of Attraction

If you can take a moment to consider the raw power that the Law of Attraction holds, then it becomes very clear that you are the sole arbiter of your life. If you aren't happy with a certain part of your life, if you feel like you suffer or feel unfulfilled, you can use the Law of Attraction to change your life.

The Law of Attraction is a philosophical concept that poses the idea that positive thoughts will bring positive outcomes to you. The idea is primarily used in goal setting, turning negative beliefs into positive beliefs, and finding your overarching purpose in life. Several principles make up the basic foundation of the Law of Attraction.

Everything is a vibration

Everything that manifests itself in your life is there because it matches the vibration from your thoughts.

Everything in the Universe is in a state of vibration. The word vibration has an unfortunate connotation that turns a lot of people off. For no reason indeed, because vibrations are based on physics. The idea that everything surrounding us, including us, is made up of vibrations, which means everything in the world is in a constant state of vibration. Even objects that appear to be stationary are in fact vibrating.

Think about the world as something you observe. You are engaging with all the energy that you come into contact with. You also create your own energy in your movements and even your thoughts and feelings. Our thoughts and feelings have a vibrational frequency. According to the Law of Attraction, like energy attracts like energy. So whether we're aware of it or not, the Universe merges with the vibrations we put out. That idea leads us to the following foundational idea.

Like attracts like

Things that are similar gravitate towards one another. That can be said for compatible couples, friend groups, event elements.

The idea is that your thoughts, attitudes, feelings, and all the other things that make up your vibrational energy will attract that which is similar. If you are putting out positive energy into the world, it will find you. If you smile at someone on the street, they very likely will smile back.

Nature hates vacuums

Building on the idea that like attracts like is the idea that nature hates vacuums. The idea is that your mind and body can never be empty, and something always has to fill up space. If you don't actively fill your mind and body with positive thoughts, it will suck in the negative. Since the mind and the body always have to be full of something, it is better to actively fill it with positivity rather than be clouded by negativity.

The present is already the best place to be

The idea that the present is already perfect is a central idea of the Law of Attraction practice.

While you might assume that because the Law of Attraction centers on looking towards the future, it would imply that there is something wrong with your life that should be changed. However, part of using the Law of Attraction focuses on the positive part of moving forward. Stay away from misery, unhappiness, or resentment towards your current situation; this clouds your energy negatively. You have to focus on the positive, which is bringing yourself good things, in order to move forward.

To use the Law of Attraction as a method of pursuing goals and desires, or even in bringing yourself closer to your ideal life, you have to carve out your own ideal reality. The idea sounds vague in theory but becomes firmer in practice. You are carving out your own reality to assist you in believing in something to bring it closer to yourself.

To do this, you have to find ways to incorporate the Law of Attraction into your daily life. This can be by,

+ Practicing gratitude.

+ Using visualization to visualize your goals.

+ Learning how to identify negative thinking and turn it into positive thinking.

- Looking for the positive side of every situation.

- Using positive affirmations.

Because the Law of Attraction is the idea that we can attract into our lives what we choose to focus on, it is necessary that you incorporate the concepts mentioned above into your practice. That is because the Law of Attraction finds that all thoughts turn into energy that comes back to you. That means if you're not practicing gratitude or if you're not actively changing your negative thoughts, then those thoughts are manifesting negative energy towards you.

Similarly, the Law of Attraction places a huge emphasis on setting goals. You need to find something to focus your mind and energy on to channel the positive energy towards what you want to bring yourself.

"It's already yours."
The Universe

Manifestation

Manifestation is a similar idea to the Law of Attraction in fact you will often hear them used interchangeably. However, while the Law of Attraction is the idea that you have to use the positive power of your thoughts to bring yourself positive experiences and things. Manifestation is based on the same idea but speaks directly to what you need to do to achieve it.

Essentially, manifestation and the Law of Attraction go hand-in-hand. Manifestation is putting your intention towards something that you hope will happen, then watching it happen in real life.

Manifestation techniques are the things you do, such as daily rituals or practices, which help you utilize the Law of Attraction to achieve your goals. In this journal more of these techniques will be explained, but they may include:

+ Visualization.

+ Using vision boards.

+ Cutting out self-limiting beliefs or thoughts.

+ Gratitude journaling.

+ Affirmations.

Manifestation techniques are the powerful tools you use to work within the Law of Attraction, they ensure that you can bring yourself the positive things you want that make up your dreams and desires. You will notice that the list above, includes some vague sounding things, like affirmations and visualization, but also, some tangible and normal things that plenty of people use every day. Journaling or using vision boards is a popular manifestation technique, and one that doesn't require a great deal of spiritual practice. Many people use vision boards or use journals to record their gratitude, goals or dreams, and may not even recognize that they are manifesting. That is because manifesting and using the Law of Attraction can be something you pursue either with or without intention. Your results will be more powerful if you conduct actions with intention, like in pursuing anything.

Everything happening in your life is a reflection of what is happening inside of you. Your world is a reflection of you. Whatever you focus on will take shape and manifest into your daily life. It's so important to know exactly how to use your manifesting power.

Putting your dreams and goals on paper can help you to manifest your desire. When you feel lost or unsure about your manifesting process, or even get frustrated, check back on your goals and insights to find guidance. Your manifesting journal is an ongoing process.

Throughout the rest of this journal, we're going to dive deeper into the Law of Attraction and Manifestation. You will receive a tangible step-by-step guide that explains specific methods and techniques you can use to approach the Law of Attraction. Overall, this journal is going to help you unpack and understand these techniques and methods and what might seem daunting will be much less so by the end of this journal. The goal here is to provide you with a firm set of options when following the Law of Attraction and using manifestation.

Steps to Manifest Your Dream Life

- GET CLEAR ON WHAT YOU WANT.
- VISUALIZE YOUR DESIRE OR DREAM LIFE.
- FEEL THE ENERGY OF YOUR DESIRE.
- USE AFFIRMATIONS TO REPLACE LIMITING BELIEFS.
- HAVE FAITH.
- KEEP YOUR VIBRATION HIGH.
- MATCH THE FREQUENCY OF THE REALITY YOU WANT.
- ALWAYS TRUST YOUR INTUITION.
- RELEASE CONTROL.
- BE PURPOSEFUL WITH YOUR THOUGHTS AND BELIEFS.
- KEEP IN MIND THAT REPETITION AND INTENTION IS KEY.
- CAREFULLY WATCH YOUR THOUGHTS - YOU ARE WHAT YOU THINK.
- ALIGN ACTIONS WITH YOUR GOALS .
- TAKE INSPIRED ACTION - HELP THE UNIVERSE MAKE IT HAPPEN.
- LET GO OF ANY RESISTANCE AND LIMITING BELIEFS.
- TRUST THE PROCESS.

How to Use the Law of Attraction and Manifestation

Think about it first

One of the most important things to do before you get started manifesting and using the Law of Attraction is to take a step back and take stock of what you want to get out of the process. You need to take your time to assess yourself and make sure that you want what you want. Manifestation is no joking matter, and you need to make sure that what you're trying to bring into your life is what you want in your life.

You also need to be specific as you possibly can in your desires, affirmations, and manifestations. That is because it's very difficult to bring a broad idea closer to yourself. You shouldn't pick things like happiness. That is too vague. You have to zone in on the things that will provide you happiness, like love or wealth. If at all possible, try to go beyond those things, which are still slightly vague in nature. When you are doing that work, you should stick with things that bring you passion and excitement. If the idea of wealth is very exciting and provides you with happiness, then that would be something worth manifesting. However, if you just want to find love because it feels like the right thing to do, then you might need to step back further and re-evaluate what you want to gain from the process.

Develop a clear mind

There is a good reason that so many people who use the Law of Attraction and manifestation are avid meditators. It is because the mind needs to be cleared before you can start on your journey of seeking to fulfill your dreams.

It is necessary to check whether you find all of your beliefs and thoughts necessary when bringing forth new desires and dreams. That is especially true when you consider that the Law of Attraction's entire point is to cleanse your mind of negative thoughts. You need to take a brief inventory of your thoughts, feelings, and ideas about the world. Think about whether they are positive. Think about whether they serve you in your long-term goals. If they don't fit or don't make you feel good, then they must be released.

Additionally, any of your own fears and anxieties are limiting and create problems when you manifest. You have to remove the fear and anxiety from your thoughts. They hold you back and should be treated as illusions. They are inhibiting your success, which you must recognize in order to pursue your goals.

After clearing your mind, which you can consider as a type of spring cleaning of the mind, you should feel more positive. You should feel less anxious and guilty. If you can fill your thoughts with positivity it smooths the road ahead and makes it an easier path forward.

Trust

You also need to develop a level of trust in the process. Many life coaches who coach in the Law of Attraction and manifestation will tell you that you need to trust the process blindly and surrender yourself to the law. That is absolutely true.

Your success in using these methods and techniques rests on your ability to believe in yourself and in the Law of Attraction. That is always difficult for beginners to achieve who have the seeds of doubt planted firmly in the back of their minds. However, it's helpful to remind yourself that the Law of Attraction and any manifestation technique is a direct product of your own ability to make it happen. If you can foster even a tiny seed of belief in yourself, then it will make it a whole lot easier to work with. Also, remember that the Law of Attraction is based on very simple beliefs and principles. You need to have the belief that your wishes will be fulfilled and that they deserve to be fulfilled.

Using visualization

There are a few different methods of visualization, and it can be interpreted across a few methods of conduct. The basic definition of visualization is that it is a mental process of forming visual-based images or interpreting visual-based ideas and then putting them into visible form. That sounds extremely vague and confusing. So, let's simplify it.

Visualization is basically mentally picturing and thinking about the things you want to come into your life or the things you wish were already in your life. Visualization is usually done during mindfulness practices like meditation. You would want to sit or lay down in a quiet place or any place in which you practice mindfulness and meditation and pair your visualization with it. You can also do visualizations while you're going to sleep, on the bus or train to work, or enjoying your morning coffee. It's an adaptable technique that can be paired with relaxing activities. You can take a bath and do visualizations or do them while you're doing light exercise. Find out what works best for you and put it into place.

If you haven't done visualization before, you may be a skeptic. However, you can think about visualization as a way you train your mind and prepare for experiencing something you want. That is extremely helpful because if you picture something coming into your life, the more likely it begins to seem that it will.

Visualization also creates a motivational mindset. It's sort of like a mental vision board, which we'll discuss later on. If you keep visualizing something, you are actively creating a mindset that wants to pursue it. You visualize the thing over and over again and begin to believe that it could enter your life, it then either becomes drawn to you, or you come upon opportunities that may make that thing happen.

Visualization additionally helps you identify what you really want. That is helpful for intention setting, which is a key element of many manifestation practices.

We're proud of you for taking this step towards manifesting your dream life.

Your new life begins here...

What Spirit Wants From You

This manifestation journal was created with love and the intention to guide you to your greatest good. At this point in your spiritual evolution, you must surround yourself with resources and teachings that support you on your journey. You were made to flourish and fly, let this message be a confirmation of your greatness.

So what should you do now?

Look inside yourself and see which areas need improving. Do you have a negative mindset that is preventing you from materializing your desires? Are your dreams struggling to manifest due to doubt, disbelief, and down days? The universe wants you to do the inner work and attend to your shadow self so that you can better yourself.

The law of attraction will work for you once you begin to work on yourself. It's only a moment of time until you break through the glass ceiling and blossom into the abundant being that you have always dreamt of being. Just trust the process and know that everything that you want is on its way to you. If you have asked and if you believe that you will receive.

Keep going and don't give up hope. No matter what challenges you face you can make it through to the other side and come out better and stronger than ever before. Your spirit guides are cheering you on as you take on this next chapter of your life, as are we. Pursue your goals and soon enough you will see that it was all worth it.

Reminder before we start

The Law of Attraction is a universal and a very powerful law. It reacts to the words you say, your thoughts and the emotions you experience. It makes endless abundance, infinite possibilities, infinite joy, and happiness possible.

Making a lifestyle change is difficult, especially when you want to alter several things at once. The tough part is committing and following through after you've decided to make a change. Making the changes you desire requires time and dedication, but you can do it. Just keep in mind that no one is flawless. It's inevitable that you'll make mistakes every now and again. Be kind to yourself. Maintain your focus on the fact that this is not a contest.

Relax and work at your own pace. Manifestation is similar to a mental workout. Just as with physical exercise, you may need to try a few different things until you find what works best for you. The more you learn about what happens when you use the Law of Attraction, the better. If you truly want to succeed, you must approach the Law of Attraction with long-term goals in mind. The adjustments you're implementing aren't intended to be transient. They are designed to be a component of a new way of living that you adopt in order to manifest your dream life.

You are constantly in the process of creating something new. The Law of Attraction, like gravity, is always in motion. It is always drawing things that are vibrationally aligned with your ideas and feelings.

Have faith in the Law of Attraction. Believe in its effectiveness. Have trust in your ability to make it happen for you. Believe in your ability to succeed. Always remember:

You are the creator of your own reality and you can have anything you want in life!

Let's get started!

Be The Energy You Want To *Attract*

Answer the Prompts Below

In order to attract abundance, wealth, success and happiness, you must first decide what you want. Questions have power. And by addressing deep questions you will get profound answers. Start by taking a few minutes to clear your mind, and get into a relaxed state. Close your eyes and take 5 deep breaths. Anything you feel an impulse to write, allow it.

Where do I see myself in one year?
....

Where do I see myself in five years?
....

Where do I see myself in ten years?
....

What is currently keeping me from living my dream life? One word:
....

What can I do to change this?
....
....
....

Is the life that I am living the life I want to be living?
....
....
....

Am I a happy person?
....
....
....

What parts of my life don't reflect who I am?

....
....
....
....

What is holding me back from fully embodying the version of
myself, who already has everything I am wishing for?

....
....
....
....

What I desire the most in my life is?

....
....
....
....

What my heart wants the most is?

....
....
....

For what must I forgive myself?

....
....
....

If I could live anywhere in the world, where would I live and why?

....

Do the people I surround myself with add any value to my life?

....
....
....
....

Am I holding onto something I need to let go of? What do I need to let go of to move to that next level in life?

....

....

....

....

Am I listening to my own heart and intuition?

....

....

....

What would I want to experience in life if money was not an issue?

....

....

....

....

....

....

....

How do I want to grow?

....

....

....

....

How does success look like to me?

....

....

....

....

....

....

....

Write down the reasons why you believe you are not successful yet. What would you do differently if you knew nobody would judge you? What is holding you back? What limiting beliefs are holding you back?

....
....
....
....
....
....
....
....
....
....
....
....
....
....

Write down more empowering and supportive beliefs you want to be a part of your new life story.

....
....
....
....
....
....
....
....
....
....
....
....
....
....

I release

What are you holding onto right now that no longer serves you? Let go of what holds you back, so you can attract more of what you really want.

....
....
....
....
....
....
....
....
....
....
....
....
....
....
....
....
....
....
....
....
....
....
....
....
....
....
....

Self Discovery

Do you love yourself? Why or why not? What do you love most about yourself?

....
....
....
....

What are the things you need to improve and work on?

....
....
....
....
....

Is everything in your life going too fast, too slow, or just right?

....
....
....
....

Where are you living right now - in the past, future, or present?

....
....
....

Are you completely and truly free?

....
....
....
....

In what areas of your life are you settling?

....
....
....
....

What makes you happy and relaxed?

....
....
....
....
....

What makes you feel motivated, inspired, and excited?

....
....
....
....
....

Have you been holding yourself back? How can you change that?

....
....
....
....
....
....

How would you like to be remembered?

....
....
....
....
....
....

Self Assessment

In the middle circle, draw yourself and/or write your name. Then answer the prompts to describe yourself. If you ask yourself the following questions, you'll raise your self-awareness and start making better decisions. Self-awareness is a key component of success.

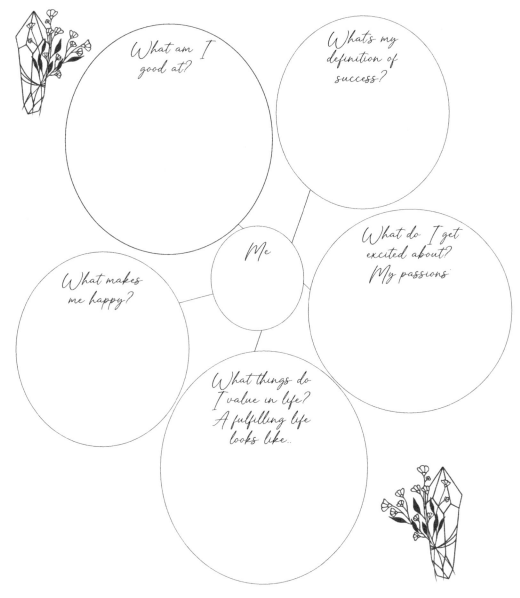

What am I good at?

What's my definition of success?

What do I get excited about? My passions

What makes me happy?

Me

What things do I value in life? A fulfilling life looks like..

Life Changes

Write down your vision of where you want to go in each level of your life and write down how you will achieve your goals. These questions will help you paint a clearer picture of what you want to do with your life.

	WHERE AM I NOW?	WHERE DO I WANT TO BE?	HOW CAN I GET THERE?
HEALTH			
SPIRITUAL			
CAREER			
RELATIONSHIP			
FAMILY			
FINANCES			
PERSONAL DEVELOPMENT			

Current Me Vs. Dream Self

There's no denying the fact that setting goals can be a daunting task, and achieving those goals is a much bigger challenge. This is where visualization exercises can come in and save the day. While they are not a guarantee that you will go to achieve goals as planned, they do a good job of helping stay focused and aligned with your desires.

"Current me vs. dream self" is a visualization exercise where you represent your current self and everything thing you are going through, as well as your ideal self. While some people prefer to draw an image of their current and ideal selves, it's not a must. You can describe the two versions of yourself on the next page.

On the left side, start writing a description of your current situation. Write about who you are right now, what you are happy with in your life, as well as your biggest challenges. Be direct in your description and avoid using unnecessary words.

On the right side, visualize your ideal self and start describing her in writing. For instance, if your goal is to become a successful business woman, your ideal self might start the day with a good mindset. You want to include things like "I read and learn constantly", "I set goals and stick to them" and so on.

Current me | Dream self

Future Self Q&A

Describe your future self. What does she look like, act like, dress like?

....
....
....
....
....
....
....
....
....
....
....
....

What does a typical day look like for her?

....
....
....
....
....
....
....
....
....
....
....
....

How does she feel about herself?

....
....
....
....
....

What habits does she have?

....
....
....
....
....
....

What are her relationships like?

....
....
....
....
....
....

What is her home and environment like?

....
....
....
....

What do people say about her?

....
....
....
....
....

Vision Board

There's something wonderful about putting your big ideas, desires, dreams and goals down on paper.

Investing time and work in creating a vision board can not only help you get clear on what you want to accomplish in your life, but it will also help your dreams come true. A vision board brings the dream to life in your imagination, allowing you to feel it is possible.

A vision board is a tangible depiction of the goals you want to attain. Having a visual reminder will assist you in remaining focused. A vision board also fosters an emotional connection that encourages you.

It's always amazing to go back and look at an old vision board and discover how many dreams have come true!

SOMETIMES YOU HAVE TO SEE IT TO BELIEVE IT!

"The biggest adventure you can take is to live the life of your dreams."

Oprah Winfrey

Vision Board

Vision board cut-outs on the last pages

Set the tone. Turn off the TV and put on some soothing music. Light a candle and make your room as uncluttered as possible. Consider the following:

* What are your most important dreams and goals?

* What will each aspect of your life look like once you've realized your dream?

* Consider your dreams in the following areas: relationships, work, finances, house, travel, personal development, and health. Your vision board should be focused on how you want to feel rather than just what you desire.

* You may also split your vision board into categories: having your vision board separated into particular categories might help you be clear on how you want your life to develop (categories can include: relationships and family, finances, career or business, health and fitness, travel, education and hobbies, spirituality and material possessions).

* Allow yourself an hour or two to put your board together without tension.

* Put anything that inspires and drives you on your vision board.

* Look for and clip out images and statements that represent your aspirations or simply speak to you. Go to the computer and perform an image search. Combine magazine photos, photographs printed from the internet, and text. Fill in the blanks with motivating positive affirmations that symbolize how you want to feel. Do not be afraid to include photographs of locations you've always dreamed of visiting as well as statements and sayings that inspire you.

* Every day, take a few moments to reflect on your vision board. At least once a day, pause and evaluate the visuals, statements, and goals.

Vision Board

Vision Board

Read out loud

I AM THE CREATOR OF MY REALITY.

I AM THE ARCHITECT OF MY LIFE.

I AM FREE OF LIMITING BELIEFS.

I AM ATTRACTING ENDLESS
ABUNDANCE INTO MY LIFE.

See Yourself Living In Abundance And You Will

Attract It

Create Your Mission Statement

A mission statement defines your purpose in life, it summarizes your values and goals. In essence, it's a statement about who you are and how you will live your life.

We all have goals (or at least we think we do) we are trying to achieve in life. But bonding them together, polishing and organizing them, and then using them to formulate a strong mission statement can make a lot of difference in your life journey.

A mission statement will help you stay focused and inspire you to put in more effort towards achieving your goals. Your mission statement will always be the driving force that continues to push you and ensure you don't take your eyes off your life's purpose.

We know the importance of visualization when it comes to the law of attraction and manifesting your heart desires. Creating a mission statement can help you envision the future and ensure it's always in your line of view. Remember you are more likely to achieve anything you constantly have your sight on. Another reason to keep a mission statement is that it can help you align your behaviors. The outcome you are trying to achieve requires small, simple, and consistent actions that keep moving you towards that goal. These small actions add up over time to gradually make your dreams a reality.

Your mission statement should contain a summary of specific actions you will be taking towards achieving your goals and purpose in life.

My Mission Statement

....
....
....
....
....
....
....
....
....
....
....
....
....
....
....
....
....
....
....
....
....
....
....
....
....
....
....
....
....

Setting Goals

This is the time for you to attract the lifestyle you want. If change is calling your name, answer! Don't get stuck in a rut, make a plan for how you're going to switch things up and reroute the direction of your life. Use our tips to guide you into making effective goals. They'll push you to become the best version of yourself and build a new and improved life for yourself.

Don't Be 'Realistic'

How many times have you had a dream only to be told that you need to be practical, sensible, and rational? Though it's often said out of love, this so-called advice can hold you back from realizing your potential. The fact of the matter is anything is possible with the law of attraction so trying to be 'realistic' could keep you from living your best life.

If you believe in yourself then you will achieve your goals and bring your dreams to life. The only limitations that exist are the ones that you have formulated in your mind. Take control! Now is the perfect moment to break through your blockages and prove to the world that you can be, do and have everything that you want.

Be Specific

When you're attempting to manifest you need to be specific about what you want. The universe likes clarity, the more detailed you are about your goals the more accurate your manifestations will become. Take money for example. Some people make the mistake of asking for more of it rather than specifying how much they want.

Setting your intention to manifest more money could mean that you receive less than what would make you happy. After all, attracting a dollar is technically manifesting more money, is it not? If you want to be successful in your life you need to know what you want and go after it!

Start by looking at your current circumstances and make a list of things that you want to change. It can include every area of your life including your health and wellness, career, friendships, and love. Get a clear picture of what you want and you can begin the process of manifesting your desires.

Have Fun

One of the most important tips that you should take into consideration is to enjoy the process. When you're determining what you want make sure that it brings you joy and have fun with the attraction process.

If something feels forced or unnatural you need to reevaluate whether or not it is right for you. Don't be afraid to question your goals if they don't bring you happiness. By removing obstacles to your success you will find the abundance that you deserve.

My Goals

Having goals is like having a map. You know where you are heading, and this gives you motivation.

SET GOALS IN ALL AREAS OF YOUR LIFE

1.

2.

3.

4.

5.

6.

7.

8.

9.

10.

Goal Setting

CHOOSE AND FOCUS ON TOP 5 GOALS FROM YOU LIST AND ASK YOURSELF - WHY ARE THESE GOALS IMPORTANT TO ME?

GOAL

1.

2.

3.

4.

5.

WHY?

REWARD YOURSELF FOR ACHIEVING YOUR GOALS

ACHIEVED

1.

2.

3.

4.

5.

REWARD

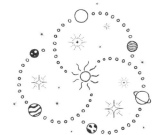

Goal Setting

Ask yourself - how will I make it happen?
Start taking action steps to achieve your goals.

MY GOAL	WHAT ARE MOST IMPORTANT STEPS TO MAKE IT HAPPEN?
	1. 2. 3. 4. 5.
	1. 2. 3. 4. 5.
	1. 2. 3. 4. 5.
	1. 2. 3. 4. 5.
	1. 2. 3. 4. 5.

Bucket List

On the left side write down or draw all the things you want to EXPERIENCE. On the right side write down or draw all the things you want to ACHIEVE.

EXPERIENCES	ACHIEVEMENTS

Affirmations

If you have been reading or learning about the law of attraction for a while, then you must have come across the term "positive affirmations." Affirmations can give you a boost and help you raise your vibration, which is a required ingredient in any manifestation process or journey. Lots of people from all walks of life have benefited immensely from the efficacy of positive affirmations.

Positive affirmations are easy to use because you only have to say them repeatedly to yourself until you begin to feel their impact in your everyday life. While most people who are familiar with the concept of manifestation know what affirmations are, it's not uncommon to still find newbies struggling to put the pieces together.

Positive affirmations are extremely powerful, short statements that you can use to fire up your confidence and raise your vibration frequently. Positive affirmations can deliver extraordinary results when used the right way. And there's no better way to use them than to align your everyday life with them. You should not just say these positive affirmations as a daily ritual, they should become a part of you and before you know it, those words will start making you a better person.

Research shows that 8 out of 10 thoughts coming out of your subconscious mind are negative, can affect the kind of life you live and the things you can manifest. Positive affirmations put you in charge of your thought process and you will be able to focus only on positive things. When you consistently say these affirmations, your subconscious mind will be left with no other choice than to accept only positive vibes and free itself from all the negative thoughts.

When you form the habit of saying positive affirmations every day, you are proactively training your mind to always reject negativity and only choose positivity. Here are some examples of affirmations you can start using to align your thoughts:

✦ I am full of different money-making ideas.

✦ I am manifesting new business opportunities and concepts every day.

✦ I am in full control of my finances.

✦ I am independent and successful.

✦ I am a source of blessing and inspiration to the people around me.

✦ I am stepping into my success and greatness this week.

✦ I am blessed beyond every reasonable doubt.

✦ I am a force to be reckoned with in every of life's endeavors.

✦ Every move I make takes me a step closer to my goal.

✦ I am attracting people with high vibrational frequency.

The key to having success with affirmations is to be consistent and never go a day without saying them. To make things easier, you can adopt them as your morning ritual. You can stand in front of the mirror every morning and say the affirmations that relate to the outcome you want to manifest.

Another thing you need to know is that having the right mindset will make these positive affirmations more effective when you use them. Remember the aim is to raise your vibration and get you closer to manifesting your dream, and it's hard to achieve without the right mentality.

Affirmations for Love

- I am loved.
- I love myself.
- I am worthy of love.
- I love my life.
- I love who I am.
- I am radiating love.
- I am open to love.
- I accept myself.
- I open my heart to love.
- I deserve love and affection.
- I feel loved fully for who I am.
- I am attracting a real connection.
- I love the way I feel about myself.
- My life is filled with love.
- My heart is prepared to receive love.
- I am worthy of the unconditional love.
- I am ready to meet my soulmate.
- I manifest love and romance into my life with ease.
- I attract loving relationships into my life.
- I am attracting a kind, loving partner.
- True love is possible for me.
- I am ready for love to change my life.
- I deserve to be happy in my relationships.
- I attract loving people into my life.
- My relationships are always fulfilling.
- What I want is coming to me.
- I am manifesting a healthy, safe, loving relationship.
- I experience love wherever I go.
- I am ready to give and receive love.
- I love myself more and more each day.

Affirmations for Self-worth

- I am a special person. There's nobody else like me.
- I am worthy. I am loved. I am enough.
- I am perfect just the way I am.
- I am blessed.
- I like who I am and who I am becoming.
- I am beautiful.
- I grow and become a better version of myself every day.
- I am whole just as I am.
- I am worthy of love.
- I am worthy of happiness.
- I am worthy of success.
- I am a successful and happy person.
- I have everything I need to succeed.
- There's nothing I need to change about myself to be accepted and loved.
- I have great potential that I tap into every day!
- I appreciate all the lessons that life has taught me.
- I believe in myself and my power.
- I deserve to be paid well for my skills.
- I have the power to create the life I want.
- I love who I am inside and out.
- I treat myself with respect.
- I have unique ideas to share with the world.
- I deserve everything I desire.
- I make a difference in the world.
- I view myself through kind eyes.
- Nothing can stop me from achieving my dreams
- I can have everything I want in life.
- I learn and grow every day.
- I am worthy of the compliments I receive.

Affirmations for Success and Wealth

- ✦ I am worthy of success, prosperity, and peace.
- ✦ I am committed to my own success.
- ✦ I believe I can do anything, but fail.
- ✦ I am full of purpose, vision, and ability.
- ✦ I am worthy of the wealth I desire.
- ✦ Every goal that I set, I accomplish.
- ✦ I walk in confidence and power.
- ✦ My potential to succeed is infinite. I fearlessly follow my dreams.
- ✦ I am chosen, valuable, and I always succeed.
- ✦ I can achieve greatness.
- ✦ Money flows to me effortlessly.
- ✦ My intellectual property is worth more than all the riches of the world.
- ✦ I am talented, creative, and original.
- ✦ I am a magnet for success.
- ✦ I am determined to take my seat at the table.
- ✦ Winning is my birthright.
- ✦ I am financially free.
- ✦ My career is a perfect fit for me. I am proud of what I accomplished.
- ✦ Nothing can stop me from achieving my dreams.
- ✦ I have the courage to create positive change in my life.
- ✦ I make bold financial decisions that work in my favor.
- ✦ I always have enough money.
- ✦ I am creative in acquiring various streams of income.
- ✦ I have unlimited resources to fuel my success.
- ✦ I love money because money loves me.
- ✦ I am a money magnet.
- ✦ Success comes naturally to me.
- ✦ My net worth is growing daily. Wealth is pouring into my life.
- ✦ Great things always seem to come my way.

Affirmations for Body Positivity

- ✦ I love myself and my body.
- ✦ I am worthy, whole and complete.
- ✦ I love my body because it's the house of a goddess.
- ✦ I feed my body healthy nourishing food.
- ✦ No one has the power to make me feel bad about myself.
- ✦ I am grateful for all the things I can do. I am grateful for my body.
- ✦ I am grateful for what my body is capable of doing.
- ✦ Others opinions of my body do not affect me.
- ✦ My opinion of myself is the only one that counts.
- ✦ I thank the food I eat for nourishing me.
- ✦ I feel strong and confident in my body.
- ✦ My worth isn't defined by my weight.
- ✦ I accept my body the way it is.
- ✦ My body is perfect the way that it is.
- ✦ I will treat my body with kindness.
- ✦ I treat my body with love and respect.
- ✦ My body deserves to be taken care of.
- ✦ I trust the wisdom of my body.
- ✦ I choose to be kind to my body.
- ✦ Food is not the enemy.
- ✦ My body is a gift.
- ✦ I am beautiful, in every single way.
- ✦ I am beautiful inside and out.
- ✦ My body is my home.
- ✦ I am confident in my body.
- ✦ I accept myself as I am.
- ✦ I love my amazing body.
- ✦ I love my body deeply and fully.
- ✦ I release my insecurities.
- ✦ I love my body as it is.

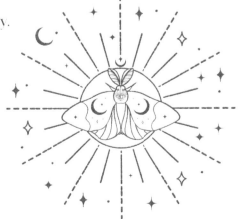

Affirmations for Abundance

- ✦ My destiny is filled with abundance.
- ✦ I deserve abundance in my life.
- ✦ I am worthy of a wealthy life.
- ✦ I am opening myself to unlimited wealth.
- ✦ I can have everything I want in life.
- ✦ I am blessed. It's natural for me to feel abundant.
- ✦ I am free to create the life I desire to live.
- ✦ I am aligned with the energy of wealth and abundance.
- ✦ I am the architect of my life.
- ✦ I live a healthy, wealthy life.
- ✦ I have an abundance mindset.
- ✦ My life is abundant.
- ✦ My income is always increasing.
- ✦ I always have everything I need.
- ✦ My goals and dreams always come true.
- ✦ I am grateful for my full, rich, and prosperous life.
- ✦ I attract miracles into my life.
- ✦ Abundance comes to me easily.
- ✦ I deserve abundance and prosperity.
- ✦ Every day I am attracting wealth and abundance.
- ✦ I stand firmly in my truth and hold my head high as I boldly make my dreams my reality.
- ✦ I am financially abundant and free.
- ✦ My network is substantial and supportive.
- ✦ My income is constantly increasing.
- ✦ I am open to receiving limitless abundance.
- ✦ I get rich doing what I love.
- ✦ Abundance is all around me.
- ✦ I am generous on every occasion. As I give, my wealth increases.
- ✦ Abundance is my birthright. I was born to be abundant.

Affirmations for Stress Relief

- My past is behind me and I am victorious.
- The past is over. I am healing. I release all past hurt.
- I feel the stress leaving my body. I am letting go of my worries.
- I am grateful for the wonderful things in my life.
- I am relaxed and calm.
- I deserve peace. My peace is my power.
- I release all negativity and focus on my own uniqueness and destiny.
- I easily overcome stressful situations.
- I have the courage to take my own unique path.
- I am led by my dreams rather than doubts.
- I am in charge of my personal happiness.
- I have the support I need.
- I do my best every day.
- I release all fears and doubts.
- I can have a new beginning.
- I have the power to overcome my fears.
- I am in the process of positive change.
- I focus on what I can control.
- Everything is going to be okay.
- I am strong and confident.
- My soul is at peace.
- I reclaim my own power. I let go of that which no longer serves me.
- I forgive myself and evict all past hurts and shame that have attached to my life.
- I am in control of my life. I am in charge of how I feel.
- I am safe and supported.
- I am in the right place at the right time.
- I embrace this journey called "life" with enthusiasm and pride.
- I am in the process of positive change.
- I cherish every opportunity to walk in my purpose.

Alignment

Make yourself an enthusiastic match for whatever it is you desire. Write down any negative self-talk, or negative remarks, and then transform your negative thoughts into positive affirmations that will help you become in sync with what you want. The more you combat negative thoughts with positive affirmations, the simpler it will be to dismiss them and, eventually, the less they will occur.

NEGATIVE SELF-TALK NEGATIVE THOUGHTS	POSITIVE AFFIRMATIONS ALIGNMENT STATEMENTS

Release Fear

You are trapped by fear, but it does not have to own you. Fear is a natural emotion that we all encounter from time to time. Because you are human, you are afraid. Write down your doubts, concerns, fears, and worries on the left side. Make a note of them as soon as they come to mind - without judgment. Now, on the right, come up with some 'antidotes' - your positive affirmations.

MY FEARS	POSITIVE AFFIRMATIONS

Fear Setting

Tim Ferriss inspired the Fear Setting practice. Fear setting is a technique for visualizing all of the awful things that may happen to you in order to reduce your fear of taking action.

How many times have you been stopped by fear of what could happen rather than acting on something you truly wanted to do?

Consider Fear Setting to be the polar opposite of Goal Setting. Make a checklist of what you are frightened to do and what you are worried will happen instead of a list of what you want to do.

"And you ask
'What if I fall?' Oh but my darling,
what if you fly?"
Erin Hanson

DEFINE What are the worst things that could happen?	PREVENT How do I prevent each from happening?	REPAIR If the worst happens, how can I fix it?	BENEFITS Possible benefits if successful	COSTS If I avoid doing this thing what might I miss out on?

Mind Maps

Mind maps are effective visual representations that help you organize your ideas. A finished mind map provides you with a higher-level view of your concepts in general. Simply jotting down all of your goals in one spot will most likely provide you with valuable insight into your life.

Begin by free-writing any ideas, feelings, or observations you have concerning your health, money, family, spirituality, relationships, vacation plans, work aspirations, and personal development objectives.

To generate ideas, consider the following:

- What is most significant to me about this part of my life, and why?
- What is the one thing I would alter if I had the chance?
- How would success ideally seem to me?

Mind Map

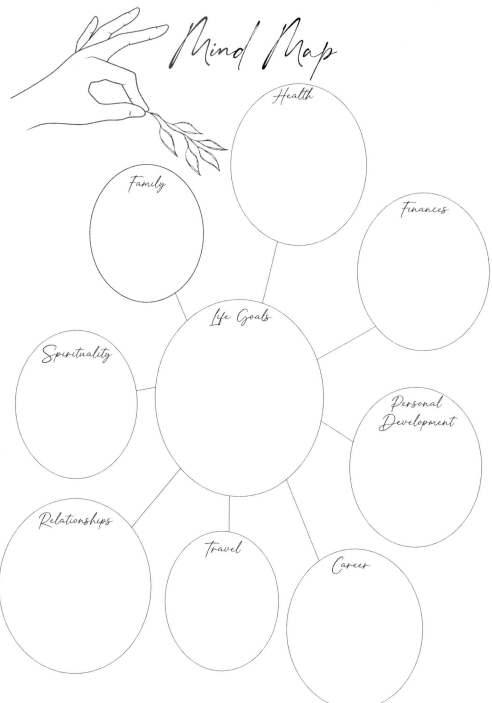

Health

Family

Finances

Life Goals

Spirituality

Personal Development

Relationships

Travel

Career

"Whatever you hold in your mind on a consistent basis is exactly what you will experience in your life."

Tony Robbins

Intentions

Setting intentions is not the same as setting goals. A goal is a strategy that you devise to accomplish something in the future. An intention is more of a guide.

Intentions are about being and goals are about doing.

Setting intentions is the act of articulating what you want to achieve with your activities. It's a commitment to the direction you want the journey to go.

Intentions are concerned with how you are being in the present moment while you work toward your goals. Setting an intention is similar to sketching a map of where you want to go. It takes on the role of the driving force behind your ambitions and visions.

"Your thoughts are the architects of your destiny."

David. O. McKays

My Intentions

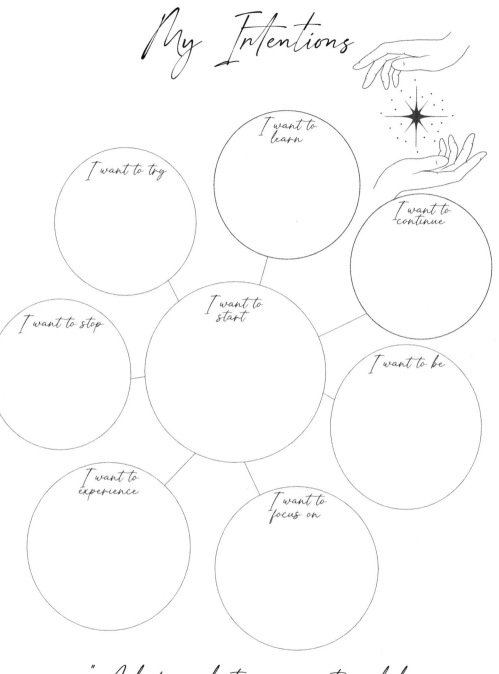

I want to try

I want to learn

I want to continue

I want to stop

I want to start

I want to be

I want to experience

I want to focus on

"Ask for what you want and be prepared to get it."

Maya Angelou

Your *Dream Life* Is Closer Than You Think

Manifesting Money

Have you ever looked at your bank account and felt frustrated? You work hard, you save up and somehow it still doesn't seem to be enough. Money is one of the most talked-about topics particularly when the law of attraction comes into play. If people can manifest love, happiness and good health with this universal law then surely money is possible, right?

The answer is absolutely! The law of attraction is the concept of 'like entering into like'. It states that everything in the universe is made of energy. Your thoughts and feelings attract specific people, life events and outcomes which match that energetic vibration. This also includes the state of your finances. So how can you use the law of attraction and what methods can you implement to manifest the wealth and abundance that you want? Read on to find out everything that you need to know...

The Key Steps to Manifesting Money with the Law of Attraction

If you want to boost your bank balance and create the lifestyle that you have always wanted you have to understand how the law of attraction works. Once you know the steps to manifesting the money you want you will transform your life in ways that you have never known. You need to familiarize yourself with the 'how to' before you start to take action so you can ensure your success.

These steps are simple, easy and straightforward to implement. With a little practice, you can go from broke to wealthy in no time at all. The law of attraction has been used by some of the biggest household names such as Oprah, Will Smith and Jim Carrey. Each one has used these exact principles to bring them immense amounts of money and fame. If they can do it then so can you.

Set your intention

If you don't know what you want, how can you ask for it? The process of conscious manifestation is the magic formula that will make your dreams come true. In the story Aladdin, the genie asks him to make three wishes. If Aladdin did not set his intention and state exactly what he wants he wouldn't have received what he wanted.

The same principle applies to you when you are seeking to manifest money. You have to know exactly what you want and communicate that to the universe. Many people who want to improve their finances will try to manifest 'more money', but what does that mean? More money could be anything from $5 to $1,000,000 so you have to be specific.

The universe takes your intentions at face value so detail is the key to ensuring that your manifestations come true. To help you clarify what you want, pick a specific amount of money and use that as your focus. The law of attraction manifests what your energy is aligned to and so you need to choose what vibration you want to connect with.

To further set your intention, write out a list of everything that you plan on spending your money on. Think about how that money could help you and focus on the benefits that it holds. Let this money become your deepest desire and that amount will surely be available to you.

Believe

Your thoughts, mindset and beliefs are what influences your experiences. Your subconscious mind is where these attributes are held which creates your reality. You have to believe with all of your heart, mind and soul that it is possible for you to have the money that you want. You are a creative being with the power to attract all of the money you could ever dream of. You need to trust in your ability and feel the universal power that flows through your veins. Nothing is too much for you to manifest.

All of your thoughts have power and so if your words are saying 'I have manifested $10,000' but your mind is thinking 'that's not possible' then you will struggle to attract the money that you want. If you know that something is possible then you remove any resistance that you may have and it can easily become part of your experience.

Take ordering from a restaurant, for example. When you sit down at your table and the waiter takes your order you don't keep reordering your meal because you are unsure that it will come. You wouldn't doubt yourself because you feel as though the restaurant won't give you your food. No. You know that as soon as you make your intention clear the information for your order will be relayed to the kitchen and the chef will start making your food.

As soon as you make your intention clear the universe sets the wheels in motion. As long as your vibration matches what you want to manifest you can be sure that it will come to you. Believing in your power sustains your manifestation, the moment that you start to question whether or not it is possible you prevent it from taking form. Now is the time to relax and believe.

Receive

This is the last stage in the manifestation process and the part where you will reach your financial goals. Imagine that you receive everything that you have been asking for. All the money that you wanted to attract has flowed into your life. Suddenly, you can now book the perfect vacation, buy that dream house and treat your loved ones. How would you feel? Excited!

To receive you need to feel as though it has already happened and feel the emotions of having it. Become the very thing that you have been asking for and celebrate your win! When you get the amount of money that you want you will feel elated and overjoyed so therefore that is exactly what you should be feeling.

Some people make the mistake of sinking into a feeling of lack. If their manifestation is taking too long they start to question the validity of the law of attraction and start wondering 'WHERE IS MY MONEY?!'. However long it takes to manifest it will work in divine timing. The moment that you start to focus on not having what you have asked for it will cease to be.

When you plant a seed in the ground you don't keep digging it up to check if it's growing. You feel good that it is on its way to you and you shower it with life-affirming water, or in your case, you continue to think positive thoughts. Be open to receiving and expect the money that you want to come to you. Don't focus on the how, just let it be and go with the flow.

Changing Your Limiting Beliefs about Money

So you now know the steps to manifesting money. The belief aspect of this theory is one of the most important parts of mastering the law of attraction for wealth. It can be the difference between staying where you are or progressing and achieving extraordinary levels of prosperity.

Your belief system is the foundation for your life. It outlines everything that you are attracting into your world. From how much money you have made in your career to those moments when you always seem to attract money at certain times, it is all down to the subconscious beliefs that you hold in your mind.

Life mastery through the law of attraction involves empowering yourself and feeding your mind with positive new beliefs. If you feel as though you are not meant to be rich then according to the law that will be your reality. If you question whether or not you deserve to be financially free you will always be kept in a position of 'just getting by'. However, if you know, trust and believe that abundance is your birthright then you will never have to worry about money again.

Shifting your beliefs is one of the best things that you can do for your self-development and your finances. When you work through your limiting beliefs it will trigger remarkable changes in your life and will affect the relationship that you have with money. When you work on yourself then the universe will work in your favor. If you want to change your money mindset then first you have to...

Identify Your Limiting Beliefs

Life isn't happening to you, it is being shaped by the many thoughts and beliefs that you express on a daily basis. We live our lives on autopilot and naturally fall into a rhythm that helps us to move from one day to the next. When you start to become aware of your beliefs and change them you effectively grab the wheel and control the direction that your life is going in. To shift your beliefs you need to work out what they are. This takes a certain amount of honesty and openness where you are able to work through the thoughts that you have toward money.

To help you make sense of what you are feeling, write out how you feel about your job, salary, the money you have in your bank account, what you heard about money growing up and any dismissive comments that anyone has made toward you about achieving your dreams. As hard as it may be, you will soon feel good about this process as it will show you what you need to work on. You may identify that the reason you are always in debt is that a parent constantly complained about owing money while you were growing up. If you have struggled with making a business work you may be holding onto negative comments made about you becoming an entrepreneur.

Whatever negative belief that you write out is exactly what you need to change. These are the beliefs that are holding you back from greatness and now is the moment that you change them forever.

Pivot Your Beliefs

Just as easily as you acquired these beliefs you can change them. Your mind is like a sponge that absorbs everything around you. Changing your thoughts toward money involves squeezing it out and soaking up fresh and positive thoughts about wealth. Taking the list of negative ideas that you have around money, write out the opposite as affirmations. For example, if your limiting belief is 'I could never be rich because I don't deserve it' then you need to flip the script to read 'I deserve to be wealthy!'

You need to create a new message for yourself, one that says I AM ABUNDANT! The new beliefs that you are writing out will become part of your psyche and will shift your connection to money in a way that benefits you entirely. This technique enables you to rewrite and reprogram your subconscious mind to adopt a healthier attitude toward money. It will give you the fuel that you need to work toward what you want and will help you to recognize that you are meant to have all of the prosperity that you could ever dream of.

As you write out your new beliefs make sure to start your sentences with 'I am' or 'I have'. When you write in the present tense you are telling the universe that it is already happening. If the universe accepts everything that you believe to the very last detail you don't want to create affirmations that exist in the past or future as you'll be continuously waiting for them to manifest.

Impress New Beliefs onto Your Mindset

Affirmations are like building blocks that help you to create the mindset that you want. Using them can be therapeutic as you challenge old, outdated thoughts toward money, however, it can also shift your point of attraction to one that expects, loves and appreciates money. By using the affirmations that you wrote to counteract your negative beliefs you can use them to create a new ritual.

This is a crucial step as it plants the seeds of abundance and cements your new and improved relationship with money. If you remove limiting beliefs you have to replace them with exactly what will help you to consistently attract money. You want to ensure that you can continue to manifest wealth and prosperity so that you can live the lifestyle that you deserve. Positive affirmations will help you to connect to your higher power and understand the truth of your being. You were always meant to be prosperous and abundant, however, your negative experiences of money that were influenced by life events, your upbringing and other aspects have impacted your ability to attract the money you desire.

Poverty can only exist in your life if you continue to entertain thoughts of poverty. Your affirmations simply dissolve these limiting beliefs and create a fresh perspective. To use them effectively, recite your affirmations in the morning. This is when your brain is the most receptive to taking in new thoughts and ideas. It will also help you become motivated and full of the energy that you need to make your dreams come true. Using affirmations in the morning is a great way to start your day. Similarly, reading your affirmations at night will reconfigure your subconscious mind during your sleep. This is a powerful time to work with your mind and develop your thoughts and feelings toward money.

"The first step to getting the things you want out of life is this - decide what you want."

Ben Stein

How to Visualize Wealth and Act as if You Are Already Wealthy

Visualization taps into the creative part of your mind. As a creator of your reality, you are using this tool every day to influence your life. When you use it in a conscious way you are deliberately inviting the money that you want to make its way toward you. Visualizing uses your imagination to focus on your goals. By creating visual sequences in your mind you tap into the energy of what you want and manifest it into your life. However, there is a particular way that can make visualization work for you. It is more than just daydreaming it uses the pure potential of the universe and harnesses the power of your mind.

If you want to manifest money, visualization can be one of the most powerful techniques that you can implement. If you can see yourself living freely with money at your disposal then you can connect with it. Visualization will free you from the confines of your current circumstances and take you to another realm where fantasy becomes reality. You can envision anything you want and tap into the feeling of happiness, bliss and joy that having the money that you want will give you. That is the magic behind visualization as it helps you to feel as though you are already wealthy.

In order to make the most out of this method, there is a secret ingredient you must use. Combined with the potential of your manifestation powers, it will almost certainly help you to attract exactly what you want. When you visualize you must always use your senses. This is absolutely vital if you want to use the law of attraction to draw the money that you want to you. During your visualization when you use your senses think about the list of things that you want to buy with this money and incorporate it into your exercise.

To visualize, close your eyes and picture yourself with the money that you want. You can imagine that it has been deposited into your bank or picture yourself spending that money. Feel the energy of your visualization from every aspect of your senses.

See the new clothes that you have bought with the money you manifested.

Hear the sound of the new car that you have bought with the money.

Feel the sand between your toes as you visualize yourself on the beach of a luxury resort.

Taste the food as you dine at a 5 star restaurant.

Smell the air in the new home that you have bought for yourself and your family.

Your senses will help your visualization to feel more real and obtainable. Once you have finished your visualization, hold on to the emotional state that it brings and use it to act as if you have already reached your financial goals. This will attract the money that you want and ensure that the universe gives you more than what you bargained for.

Gratitude

If you want more money in your life you need to appreciate what you already have. Gratitude is incredibly powerful. If you have enough of it you will be granted more money and if you do not have enough you will notice that unexpected bills and money problems will suddenly become part of your experience. The magic words 'thank you' can give you everything that you want and more. As they say, it's better to lose count while naming your blessings than to lose your blessings to counting your troubles.

When you feel as though you don't have enough money you tend to focus on it and due to the law of attraction you will attract more circumstances that take money away from you. It can feel like an endless cycle that drags you into having more issues with money. However, gratitude helps you to feel good about what you have. Whether it's your job, business or any little bit of money that comes your way, saying 'thank you' will make you feel better in the long run and consequently will manifest more reasons to be thankful.

Say 'thank you' everywhere you go and mean it. If you get a discount on something then give thanks. If you find a penny on the ground then appreciate it. When you receive your paycheck feel good because you have money coming in. Even if you don't have any money in your bank account, feel grateful for all the times that you had money in the past.

There is always a reason to be grateful and your gratitude should not depend on whether or not you already have what you want.

To help you attract money and focus on the positive financial aspects in your life, start writing a gratitude list. Any time that you receive money write it out in a journal. Even when a bill comes in the post, think about the service that was available to you and feel grateful. As you slowly start to incorporate gratitude into your life you will feel better about money and you will receive more abundance in the process.

You can have as much money as your heart desires. It is up to you to create the reality that you want. You are like a magnet that attracts or repels money and so it is within your power to manifest the life that you truly deserve. Fill your life with light and love, in return, you will receive abundance and prosperity.

"The law of attraction is really obedient. When you think of the things that you want, and you focus on them with all of your intention, the law of attraction will give you what you want every time."

Lisa Nichols

Dream Life Cost Calculator

How much is it going to cost you to live your dream life? How much do you actually need to make to get there? If you want to live your dream life, you need to calculate how much it will cost you.

CATEGORY	COST
HOME	
FOOD	
SHOPPING	
UTILITIES	
HOUSEHOLD	
TRANSPORTATION	
HOBBIES	
VACATION	
FITNESS/WELLNESS	
DINING OUT	
GIFTS	

Monthly total..........................Yearly total..........................

My Dream Life

I AM ATTRACTING THE LIFESTYLE OF MY DREAMS WITH EASE AND CLARITY.

I AM WORTHY.

I AM PASSIONATE.

I AM CONFIDENT.

I AM VALUABLE.

I AM ABUNDANT.

THIS DREAM LIFE IS POSSIBLE FOR ME.

I EASILY ATTRACT (YOUR MONTHLY TOTAL) _____ EVERY MONTH, THROUGH (HOW? YOUR DREAM BUSINESS / YOUR JOB)

_____

I AM WORTHY AND DESERVING OF RECEIVING ALL THINGS ABUNDANT IN LIFE.

I AM WORTHY AND DESERVING OF AN AMAZING LIFE.

. . . .

YOUR SIGNATURE

Habits

A habit is a pattern of behavior that is repeated on a regular basis. This behavior might take the form of action, a routine, or a way of life. What you do again and again shapes who you are.

Today, your life is simply the sum of your behaviors. As a result of your behaviors, how fit or out of shape are you? As a result of your behaviors, how successful or unsuccessful are you?

To choose which habit adjustments to undertake, first do an audit of your everyday activities. Take note of how you spend your time, energy, and attention. The most effective strategy to modify undesirable behaviors is to replace them with new ones. Begin with tiny, simple modifications that you can implement on a daily basis. Celebrate every time you succeed in your habit! Feeling happy aids your brain's ability to wire in new actions, making them more likely to be repeated automatically. Good Habits to Transform Your Life:

- ✦ Journal.
- ✦ Exercise.
- ✦ Go offline.
- ✦ Spread kindness.
- ✦ Practice gratitude.
- ✦ Eat a balanced diet.
- ✦ Drink plenty of water.
- ✦ Learn something new.
- ✦ Practice mindful living.
- ✦ Read thoughtful books.
- ✦ Use positive affirmations.
- ✦ Practice daily meditation.
- ✦ Spend some time outdoors.
- ✦ Develop a healthy sleep routine

Designing Your Habits

HABITS TO BREAK	YOUR IDEAL HABITS	WHAT WILL YOUR FUTURE SELF TELL YOU, IF YOU DON'T START WITH THIS NOW?

Eliminate Excuses

Stop with the excuses - it's time to make a change. Like all bad habits, excuses are easy. They allow us to box ourselves into our comfort zone and be "okay" with our life. The excuses we use are not always something that we intentionally do. Sometimes they get the best of us, and we are not even aware of the consequences. If you want to achieve happiness in your life, and feel good with yourself, you need to stop with the excuses and start doing things instead. Become unstoppable by eliminating excuses.

YOUR EXCUSES	WHAT YOU WILL DO INSTEAD

Monthly Habit Tracker

" In essence, if we want to direct our lives, we must take control of our consistent actions. Its not what we do once in a while that shapes our lives, but what we do consistently."

Tony Robbins

Monthly Habits:

COLOR

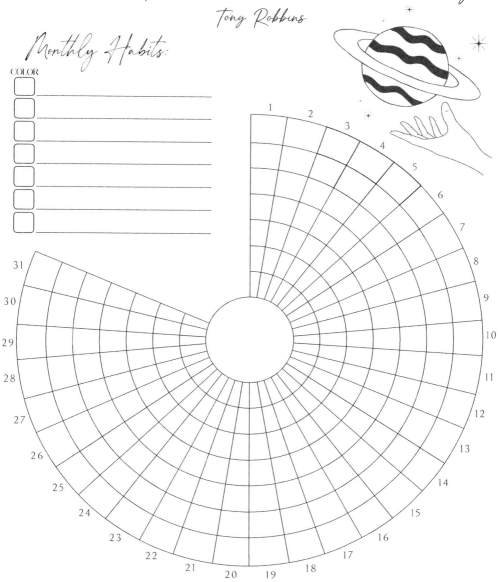

Monthly Mood Tracker

Our Mood Tracker is a powerful and simple tool for tracking your emotions - or moods - on a regular basis. You aspire to have a happy and meaningful existence. With the Mood Tracker, all of that becomes much easier.

With our Mood Tracker, you may track your triggers, look at your ups and downs, and give yourself permission to feel in order to better understand your anxiety, aid in stress reduction and become a happier person in general.

You may be able to identify events or periods when your mood rises or falls by recording your emotions. Such occurrences are frequently referred to as triggers. For example, if you observe that you become depressed whenever you visit your parents, it's significant knowledge that you can use to better understand yourself. Daily emotional reflection allows you to develop insight into the patterns of your moods, triggers, coping strategies, and perspectives. Reflect on emotions daily - gain insight into the patterns of your moods, triggers, coping skills, and mindsets.

Keep track of your feelings. Relieve your stress.

Create a happier you!

Monthly Mood Tracker

HAPPY

SAD

TIRED

MOTIVATED

SICK

FOCUSED

STRESSED

EXCITED

ANGRY

ANXIOUS

COLOR YOUR MOOD

MONTH: _____

1

8

2

7

17

12

6

25

24

14

4

23

20

31

30

10

29

5

19

21

27

15

18

11

3

26

13

16

9

28

22

Scripting

Scripting is a fun and one of the best Law of Attraction techniques out there!

Scripting is a Law of Attraction technique where you write a story about your life based on how you want it to be. This technique really gets you into character and makes your manifestation so much easier!

When scripting you write story as if it has already happened, focusing on how you would feel when your desire manifested.

Rather than writing what you want to happen, you write as if it's already happening. The point is to get excited and to feel good. Close your eyes and see what you want to manifest. Visualize your dream life or goal. Imagine every aspect of your desire and see yourself with it. Try to be as specific as possible. The more you feel as if you're living it, the more excited you get and the higher your vibration will be. When you release those high vibrations, you attract them right back to you. Scripting works so well because your are not only focusing on what you want to manifest, but how it makes you feel, and showing gratitude for it.

Read your script regularly and you'll bring your vibrational energy into alignment with your desires, causing them to manifest in your life.

Never forget:

You Are
the Creator
Of
Your Own
Reality

Scripting

Scripting is a manifestation technique that involves writing explicitly about the new reality you want to manifest. There has been a good deal of social media popularity surrounding scripting recently because a lot of people use the technique for spiritual activities in which you visit a reality while dreaming, which is called shifting. Shifting is when you essentially raise your vibration high enough that you can jump or shift through different realities. Primarily the reality you have set an intention for by scripting it in detail in this journal. This sounds like a movie or a play script which is essentially what it is. You write out your entire desired reality. You write your personal details, the world you live in, who your friends are, who your family is, what you do in a day.

So, are there any rules?

Scripting is very personalized and what makes your best script will be unique to you. However, there are some things we recommend.

1. Use the present tense in your script.

2. This puts the energy out that the desire you're wishing to attract is already yours - because it is! The key is to put yourself in the shoes of your future self and write from the perspective of that version of you.

3. It should be explicitly clear and detailed.

4. Don't ever be worried that you're being too detailed, the more detail you can provide the better. This clarifies your

manifestations. For example, if you are trying to script your ideal home you should get as specific as possible, describing every small aspect of the house. That doesn't mean you should obsess or worry over the details, but more so, lay them all out.

5. Record your feelings associated with manifesting.

6. Make note of what it feels like to have it. Do you feel a sense of pride because you have achieved something? Do you feel peaceful? Do you feel immense joy?

7. Additionally, don't forget to script your gratitude for having manifested your dream or goal. Just as you practice gratitude in every aspect of your manifestation it should be expressed in your scripting.

8. It should be realistic.

While in scripting when trying to reality shift it might be okay to embellish or script living in magical world, in fact many people have created a trend of reality shifting to Hogwarts from the Harry Potter Series, in real life it won't serve you in achieving your goals. If you want to try reality shifting, you should absolutely do so! However, for the purpose of scripting you really need to ground your desires in reality. You can't script, I have a unicorn, because you likely won't get one. Though if you do please write to us. :) Make it believable. The more you believe it's possible, the faster you'll see results.

Keep scripting light hearted and go with the flow. Enjoy every bit of the process, and let your mind and imagination to do all the talking.

Journal as if you're living that dream life, have that dream house (or whatever intention you set). Dream big! Be detailed! This is your time to really explore and journal out what reality looks and feels like!

You are the creator of your own reality. You are the writer and you can tell your story exactly as you want.

Scripting Example

Approach scripting with a free, playful attitude.

Have fun with it!

The date is important - you will be able to go back later on and see it all manifested!

Date: Monday, July 31, 2022

Write as it already happened

I am so happy and grateful now that I am living in abundance of great health, increasing wealth and thriving relationships. I am so grateful that I have goals to motivate me, dreams to inspire me and purpose to fuel me.

Life is so good right now!

Write in present tense

Thank you Universe!

Express gratitude

Tune in to your imaginative side

Speak as if It Has Already Happened and *it will...*

Script your ideal month

Date..

I am so happy and grateful now that ....

....

....

....

....

....

....

....

....

....

....

....

....

....

....

....

....

....

....

....

....

....

Script your ideal year

Date..

I am so happy and grateful now that..

....

....

....

....

....

....

....

....

....

....

....

....

....

....

....

....

....

....

....

....

Script your dream job

Date...

I am so happy and grateful now that
....
....
....
....
....
....
....
....
....
....
....
....
....
....
....
....
....
....
....
....
....
....
....
....

Script your ideal partner or relationship

Date ....

I am so happy and grateful now that ....

....

....

....

....

....

....

....

....

....

....

....

....

....

....

....

....

....

....

....

....

....

Script your ideal mindset

Date..

I am so happy and grateful now that.....................................

....

....

....

....

....

....

....

....

....

....

....

....

....

....

....

....

....

....

....

....

....

....

Script your dream home

Date ....

I am so happy and grateful now that ....

....

....

....

....

....

....

....

....

....

....

....

....

....

....

....

....

....

....

....

....

....

....

....

....

Script your ideal body

Date ....

I am so happy and grateful now that ....

....

....

....

....

....

....

....

....

....

....

....

....

....

....

....

....

....

....

....

....

....

....

Script your dream vacation.

Date ....

I am so happy and grateful now that ....

....

....

....

....

....

....

....

....

....

....

....

....

....

....

....

....

....

....

....

....

Script your dream life

Date..

I am so happy and grateful now that...............................

....

....

....

....

....

....

....

....

....

....

....

....

....

....

....

....

....

....

....

....

....

....

....

....

Read out loud

I AM OPEN TO RECEIVE.

I AM IN CHARGE OF MY LIFE.

I AM STEPPING INTO THE MOST
SUCCESSFUL DECADE OF MY LIFE.

I AM IN ALIGNMENT WITH MY SOUL
PURPOSE.

What You Feel You Will *Attract*

Kindness Log

Write down random acts of kindness. When you treat others with kindness and as you wish to be treated, that's what you receive in return.

Gratitude Board

A gratitude board is an easy and beautiful way to show what we are most grateful for. You can add images and make notes about the things that you are already grateful for.

Gratitude is a superpower emotion, practicing gratitude on a daily basis can drastically increase your quality of life.

Creating a gratitude board will help you stay focused on the positive. A gratitude board helps keep you grounded in the moment, thankful for what you already have in life while looking forward to your dreams. In fact, gratitude plays a big role in every aspect of your life.

"Be thankful for what you have; you'll end up having more. If you concentrate on what you don't have, you will never, ever have enough."

Oprah Winfrey

Gratitude Board

Gratitude Board

Gratitude Journaling

Gratitude journaling is one of the most powerful manifestation exercises. The benefits and the effects are almost endless and can be felt in nearly all areas of your life. Taking the time to write down everything you are grateful for can improve your self-esteem, help you feel relaxed and sleep better, help you stay positive, make you happier, reduce stress, and help keep your vibrational frequency on a high.

Gratitude journaling becomes more fun when you make it a habit. Since you will be making daily entries for the next 4 weeks, it's good to choose a certain time when you will make your entry each day.

It's now time to start making your entries. There are several gratitude journal prompts that can inspire what you write in your journal every day for the next 4 weeks. You can look at some of the prompts below for ideas:

✦ Looking outside your window, mention some of the things you can see and are thankful for.

✦ Think of the unique abilities you have.

✦ Think about a kind gesture from a friend or loved one.

✦ Think of those things that put a smile on your face in the past few days

✦ Try to remember a particular time when you helped someone in need.

✦ Mention someone who once rendered unsolicited help to you.

✦ Be thankful for the opportunity to see another day.

- Be grateful for the gift of a sound body and mind.
- Pull out a random photo and highlight why you cherish that moment.

You can also write about your coworkers, your business or job, your favorite food, your city or neighborhood, the current season, an unexpected event that happened, etc.

At the end of the day, there are endless possibilities when it comes to finding ideas to put in your journal. Just make sure you are making at least one entry each day for the next 4 weeks and, most importantly, have fun doing it. Here is an example:

Date   Thursday August 17

Today I am grateful for

1. Waking up this morning alive and healthy
2. My strong and capable body
3. Coming home to my excited dog

Date   Friday August 18

Today I am grateful for

1. The comfort of my home
2. Reading a message from my best friend
3. The wind blowing through the leaves

Highlights of the week

Looking at old photo albums with the family on Sunday
Watching the sunset
Getting a drink and catching up with an old friend
Nail appointment with mom
Doubled my previously highest weekly income (omg!)

Date

Today I am grateful for:

....
....
....

Date

Today I am grateful for:

....
....
....

Date

Today I am grateful for:

....
....
....

Date

Today I am grateful for:

....
....
....

Date

Today I am grateful for:

....

....

....

Date

Today I am grateful for:

....

....

....

Date

Today I am grateful for:

....

....

....

Highlights of the week

....

....

....

....

....

Date

Today I am grateful for:

....
....
....

Date

Today I am grateful for:

....
....
....

Date

Today I am grateful for:

....
....
....

Date

Today I am grateful for:

....
....
....

Date _____

Today I am grateful for:

....
....
....

Date _____

Today I am grateful for:

....
....
....

Date _____

Today I am grateful for:

....
....
....

Highlights of the week

....
....
....
....
....
....

Date

Today I am grateful for:

....
....
....

Date

Today I am grateful for:

....
....
....

Date

Today I am grateful for:

....
....
....

Date

Today I am grateful for:

....
....
....

Date

Today I am grateful for:

....
....
....

Date

Today I am grateful for:

....
....
....

Date

Today I am grateful for:

....
....
....

Highlights of the week

Date

Today I am grateful for:

....
....
....

Date

Today I am grateful for:

....
....
....

Date

Today I am grateful for:

....
....
....

Date

Today I am grateful for:

....
....
....

Date

Today I am grateful for:

....
....
....

Date

Today I am grateful for:

....
....
....

Date

Today I am grateful for:

....
....
....

Highlights of the week

....
....
....
....
....

Morning Pages

We all face different challenges in our day-to-day life. We are constantly under pressure and trying to meet certain expectations. Maybe it's your bills, lover, family, school, job, or other pursuits. The bottom line is that you have a lot of things on your mind that probably keep you awake for a moment at night now and then.

Morning pages are three pages of stream-of-consciousness writing done in the morning, typically encouraged to be in longhand. Longhand means that your pages are written in your ordinary handwriting, and stream of consciousness is simply your thoughts and reactions in a continuous flow.

Morning pages are not meant to be typed, they're not meant to be strategized, and they really do serve you the best when they're done as early in the day as possible.

Write whatever comes to your mind. It's called consciousness writing after all. Find a comfortable position and start writing. The key here is ensuring you complete the three pages whether you are motivated or not. Don't worry too much about what you are writing down, you can write about anything your dreams, goals, your worries, the sky, your dog, the meal at the restaurant, and so on.

Morning pages can help you break free from all the burden weighing you down and prepare your mind to receive and achieve what you have set out to accomplish. You will be able to rise above the voice within you, especially the ones making you doubt yourself.

Date..

Read out loud

I AM DIVINELY GUIDED AND
PROTECTED AT ALL TIMES.

I AM FREE FROM DOUBT AND WORRY.

I EFFORTLESSLY ATTRACT UNLIMITED
ABUNDANCE.

Thoughts Become Things

5x55
Manifestation Method

The 5x55 manifestation technique works by using your unconscious mind to align the vibrational frequency of your intention. It's simply done by repeating a specific affirmation 55 times for 5 consecutive days.

The meaning of 555 in numerology

The significance of the number 555 in numerology is a contributing factor to the effectiveness of the 5x55 technique. If we analyze what the number 555 means in numerology, we'll realize that it contains three digits that are repeated.

The number 5 is a symbol of change, adjustment, and transformation. So, when you focus on the number 5 while trying to manifest a specific outcome, you are aligning with the sacred energy of this powerful number.

How to use the 5x55 manifestation technique

This manifestation method, when done correctly, helps to influence your energy vibrations, and it can deliver fast results, which makes it one of the most popular manifestation techniques out there. This method will only take you 5 days to complete.

STEP 1
Choose an affirmation

After you decide on the outcome you want to manifest, the next thing is to pick an affirmation that best relates to that outcome. You can only use one affirmation with this method, so you can start by writing down five affirmations and then cut it down to one.

Make sure the affirmation you choose is simple and short, but long enough to contain the specific thing you want to manifest.

Examples are:

" I am grateful to the universe for sending me a check of $150."

" I am blessed to have lost 7 pounds in 8 days."

STEP 2
Be in the right mood

Make sure you are in a good mood and ensure nothing disturbs you. Also, you need to choose the times on all 5 days when you will be free. You will need to allocate about 20-30 minutes each day for this exercise, although it depends on how fast you can write your affirmation 55 times.

STEP 3
Start writing

Make sure you are using a real pen, not a pencil. You will need to write down your chosen affirmation 55 times and then repeat the process for 5 consecutive days.

When witting the affirmation, it's important to stay relaxed and keep your mind fixed on the outcome you are trying to manifest. You don't want any form of distraction at these critical times. You can also say the affirmations aloud while writing.

STEP 4
Take your mind off it

After completing the five days of writing, you need to take your mind off the entire process and focus on something else. Don't start obsessing over the outcome you are trying to manifest as this might allow unbelief to set in. the last thing you want to be doing at this stage is worrying about when your manifestation will take place.

You want to stop thinking about the whole process. You've done your part diligently and faithfully. It's now time to leave the universe to do its part in due time. The key is to hold trust and peace to welcome anything that comes to you. Remember:

the Universe always has your back!
Have faith! Trust! Let go!

Expect
To Manifest
Everything
That You
Want To
Manifest

DAY 1

DATE:

MANIFESTATION INTENTION:

1.
2.
3.
4.
5.
6.
7.
8.
9.
10.
11.
12.
13.
14.
15.
16.
17
18.
19.
20.
21.
22.
23.
24.
25.

26.

27.

28.

29.

30.

31.

32.

33.

34.

35.

36.

37.

38.

39.

40.

41.

42.

43.

44.

45.

46.

47.

48.

49.

50.

51.

52.

53.

54.

55.

DAY 2
DATE:

MANIFESTATION INTENTION:

1.
2.
3.
4.
5.
6.
7.
8.
9.
10.
11.
12.
13.
14.
15.
16.
17
18.
19.
20.
21.
22.
23.
24.
25.

26.

27.

28.

29.

30.

31.

32.

33.

34.

35.

36.

37.

38.

39.

40.

41.

42.

43.

44.

45.

46.

47.

48.

49.

50.

51.

52.

53.

54.

55.

DAY 3
DATE:

MANIFESTATION INTENTION:

1.
2.
3.
4.
5.
6.
7.
8.
9.
10.
11.
12.
13.
14.
15.
16.
17
18.
19.
20.
21.
22.
23.
24.
25.

26.

27.

28.

29.

30.

31.

32.

33.

34.

35.

36.

37.

38.

39.

40.

41.

42.

43.

44.

45.

46.

47.

48.

49.

50.

51.

52.

53.

54.

55.

DAY 4
DATE:

MANIFESTATION INTENTION:

1.
2.
3.
4.
5.
6.
7.
8.
9.
10.
11.
12.
13.
14.
15.
16.
17
18.
19.
20.
21.
22.
23.
24.
25.

26.

27.

28.

29.

30.

31.

32.

33.

34.

35.

36.

37.

38.

39.

40.

41.

42.

43.

44.

45.

46.

47.

48.

49.

50.

51.

52.

53.

54.

55.

DAY 5

DATE:

MANIFESTATION INTENTION:

1.
2.
3.
4.
5.
6.
7.
8.
9.
10.
11.
12.
13.
14.
15.
16.
17
18.
19.
20.
21.
22.
23.
24.
25.

26.

27.

28.

29.

30.

31.

32.

33.

34.

35.

36.

37.

38.

39.

40.

41.

42.

43.

44.

45.

46.

47.

48.

49.

50.

51.

52.

53.

54.

55.

Read out loud

I AM CAPABLE.

I AM SUCCESSFUL.

I AM IN CHARGE OF MY LIFE.

I AM MANIFESTING MY DREAMS INTO
REALITY AND CREATING THE LIFE I
DESERVE TO LIVE.

Manifestation Success Story

Use this page to write, illustrate or attach photos, receipts, evidence or proof of your 5x55 Manifestation Success Story. This will help to document your manifesting journey and minimize resistance to future manifestation and the Law of Attraction.

Act As If

Acting "as if" is one of the oldest manifestation methods and it remains one of the most effective techniques in the law of attraction. Once you master the act of "acting as if," it opens up doors of possibilities. Imagine being in a state of mind where anything is possible because you believe you can achieve whatever you focus on.

Acting "as if" simply means acting as if you already have what you are trying to manifest. While it sounds so simple to the ears, in reality, you need to take a series of proactive steps and train your mind to accept that you already have what you are trying to get from the universe.

Even if you've never come across the term "Acting as if," you've probably come across the term "fake it till you make." While faking it till you make it might not be the best way to represent "acting as if," it's the closest thing to it and the difference between the two terms lies in the mindset of the person.

Both sentiments, however, have their roots in the law of attraction and the principle of manifestation, which is simply using your mind, actions, and thoughts to accomplish your dreams and fulfill your heart's desires. So, instead of expelling all your energy chasing your dream, you simply refocus that energy and begin to act like that dream has been fulfilled already.

Can acting 'as if' change your life?

We all know that one of the main principles of the law of attraction is that once you focus all your energy and thoughts on achieving a certain goal, fulfilling your dream, or manifesting a specific outcome, you will eventually see that dream coming true before your eyes.

One of the reasons this happens is that everything in the universe is made of energy, and that includes that financial blessing, that dream car of yours, or that high-paying job you desire so much. So, when you focus on those specific things, your energy aligns with that of the universe and before you know it, the universe makes your dream come true.

You also need to understand that whatever you send into the world in the form of energy comes back to you.

So, when you start talking, acting, and carrying yourself as if you already have everything your heart desires, you will notice that those things will eventually become yours because the universe will send them your way.

Also, doing this triggers a change in your mentality and perceptions, which open up new opportunities and possibilities, and you will then notice that your dreams and aspirations become clearer. You begin to see new opportunities that your eyes were never opened to previously.

A real-life example of "acting as if" is this: let's assume you are trying to manifest a new car, you can go to a car rental and hire one for the day, or you can take a trip to the auto shop, locate your favorite car and check it out. You can sit inside, handle the steering and have a feel of the interior. That way, you are aligning your intention and vibrational frequency with that of your dream car.

How to use the "act as if" technique to manifest your desires

First, you need to identify how someone who has manifested what you want to achieve would behave. Take some of those behaviors and start acting that way. Perform the actions regularly with faith and belief in your heart.

Act every day as if you have already achieved the outcome you seek and watch how your perception of situations and the world around you changes.

When you are presented with a situation, you should pause and ask yourself, okay, how would someone with a positive mindset react to this? That is the simplest way you can begin to "act as if" you already are a person living with a more positive mindset. Think to yourself, how would a person with a positive outlook converse with people? How would a person with a positive mindset spend their day? And then do those things. It makes you more self-aware and able to develop an awareness of yourself in your conversations.

The key with the "act as if" method is that it is based on energy, as is all manifestation. So, essentially you are acting as if you already embody positive energy. If you embody this approach, you will find yourself with positive energy.

While acting as if you are already living your dream, it's time to also start showing it in your words. Words are powerful and you can use them to create whatever future you want for yourself.

Speak with authority and like someone who has already accomplished the specific outcome you wrote down in step 1 and you will leave the universe with no other choice than to make your dream come true.

You have to believe in the process of the massive change that is about to take place in your life.

As you act in your new role, you need to believe that what you want is already yours or, at least, that you are capable of reaching that goal. Once you start acting and believing in the energy of creation, you should see..

your desires becoming reality soon..

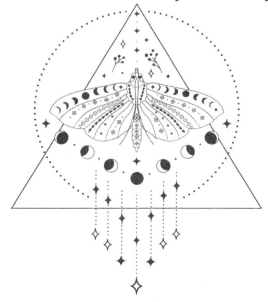

I DREAM.

I BELIEVE.

I RECEIVE.

17 Second Manifestation Technique

If you are looking to manifest something super specific, such as a specific amount of real spendable cash, a gadget, or a text or call from a specific person, this may be a manifestation method you want to try.

Perhaps the best thing about the 17-second manifestation is the fact it doesn't take your time; it can be completed quickly and you'll still have enough time to focus on other tasks. Just as the name implies, this technique only requires about 17 seconds of your time.

While you only require a few seconds for this technique, your concentration level needs to be high when carrying it out. Remember you only have 17 seconds, so the last thing you want in that period is some unnecessary distractions.

Before you start this manifestation method, it's important to ensure your vibrational energy is on the high side. Otherwise, you may have a hard time pulling it off successfully.

This technique is so short and effective that once you get it right, it will probably become your number one manifestation technique. That's how simple and effective it is.

"It's already yours."

The Universe

How to perform the 17-second manifestation technique

STEP 1
Be as relaxed as possible

You want to stay in a calm position and focus your energy on the task at hand. You also want to make sure your vibrational energy is at its highest at this point. One of the best ways to get into a relaxed mood quickly is by taking deep breaths and entering a mode of meditation.

STEP 2
Decide on the outcome you want to manifest

Take a few moments to think of the outcome you want to manifest. Since you've only got 17 seconds for this exercise, you want to be sure you are not wasting a second of that trying to decide on what you want manifest.

STEP 3
Set your timer for 17 seconds

Any device is fine as long as it allows you to set a timer a phone, stopwatch, or clock. Now, while in a perfectly relaxed mood, and for the next 17 seconds, focus on the outcome you are trying to manifest.

STEP 4

Affirm the outcome to yourself repeatedly during those 17 seconds

For instance, if you want to manifest a financial breakthrough, you can use an affirmation like "I am stepping into financial abundance." You can end the session when the timer stops.

STEP 5

Take your mind off it

This seems to be the most challenging step. After completing the 17-second exercise, you need to take your mind off everything and focus on something else. This way, you are sending a signal to the universe that you have completed your part.

369
Manifestation Method

When it comes to manifestation methods, the 369 technique is probably one of the most straightforward exercises you can do, and most importantly, it works.

The 369 manifestation technique is all about writing down your desire three times in the morning, six times in the afternoon, and nine times before retiring to your bed at night. While it may look so easy, there's a spiritual significance to the numbers 3, 6, and 9, which is what makes the method so effective.

The meaning of 369 in numerology

The number comprises three digits, each having a specific meaning and significance in numerology. The number 369 carries the combined vibrational energy of the three digits.

✦ The number 3 is a symbol of our connection to the universe or the source of creation.

✦ The number 6 symbolizes our inner harmony and strength

✦ The number 9 stands for a new birth (releasing the life we no longer want and stepping into a new life or dimension)

How to use the 369 manifestation technique

While this step seems simple, you still need to ensure you are specific with what you are trying to manifest. So, think of what outcome you want to manifest before you even get started with this technique.

Once you've figured out your outcome, it's time to put the outcome into a powerful affirmation. For instance, if you are trying to manifest a specific amount of money, you can write something like "I am so grateful I manifested $1000 in one week." Apply the 17-second rule while writing your affirmation (it should take you at least 17 seconds to write it down because it connects your written word to the subconscious mind).

STEP 1

Write down your affirmation three times in the morning as soon you are out of bed.

STEP 2

Write the same affirmation six times in the afternoon.

STEP 3

Before going to bed at night, write down the affirmation nine times.

Those are the steps outlined for you. But keep in mind that while writing your affirmations, you need to trust the universe to make it work. You can continue this method for as long as you like.

369

MORNING OF __ / __ / __

1. ....
2. ....
3. ....

WHAT ACTIONS WILL I TAKE TODAY TO ATTRACT IT?

1. ....
2. ....
3. ....

Read out loud

I AM OPEN AND READY TO ATTRACT ABUNDANCE INTO MY LIFE

369

AFTERNOON OF __/__/__

1.

2.

3.

4.

5.

6.

NIGHT OF __/__/__

1.

2.

3.

4.

5.

6.

7.

8.

9.

MORNING OF __/__/__

1. ....
2. ....
3. ....

WHAT ACTIONS WILL I TAKE TODAY TO ATTRACT IT?

1. ....
2. ....
3. ....

Read out loud

I EASILY ATTRACT THE THINGS THAT I DESIRE MOST

AFTERNOON OF __/__/__

1.
2.
3.
4.
5.
6.

NIGHT OF __/__/__

1.
2.
3.
4.
5.
6.
7.
8.
9.

MORNING OF __/__/__

1. ....
2. ....
3. ....

WHAT ACTIONS WILL I TAKE TODAY TO ATTRACT IT?

1. ....
2. ....
3. ....

Read out loud

I AM FILLED WITH LIMITLESS POTENTIAL

AFTERNOON OF __/__/__

1.
2.
3.
4.
5.
6.

NIGHT OF __/__/__

1.
2.
3.
4.
5.
6.
7.
8.
9.

MORNING OF __/__/__

1. ....
2. ....
3. ....

WHAT ACTIONS WILL I TAKE TODAY TO ATTRACT IT?

1. ....
2. ....
3. ....

Read out loud

EVERY DAY I AM MOVING TOWARDS MY BEST LIFE

AFTERNOON OF __/__/__

1.
2.
3.
4.
5.
6.

NIGHT OF __/__/__

1.
2.
3.
4.
5.
6.
7.
8.
9.

MORNING OF ___/___/___

1. ....
2. ....
3. ....

WHAT ACTIONS WILL I TAKE TODAY TO ATTRACT IT?

1. ....
2. ....
3. ....

Read out loud

I AM CREATING A LIFE OF PASSION AND PURPOSE

AFTERNOON OF __/__/__

1.
2.
3.
4.
5.
6.

NIGHT OF __/__/__

1.
2.
3.
4.
5.
6.
7.
8.
9.

Write it down

I AM MANIFESTING MY DREAMS INTO REALITY

I AM
....

I AM
....

I AM
....

I AM
....

I AM
....

I AM
....

I AM
....

I AM
....

I AM
....

Manifestation Success Story

Use this page to write, illustrate or attach photos, receipts, evidence or proof of your 369 Manifestation Success Story. This will help to document your manifesting journey and minimize resistance to future manifestation and the Law of Attraction.

The
Universe
Supports
Me

Release Your Worries

Do yourself a favor and stop obsessing over things you can't control. If you're worried about anything in your life, write down everything you're worried about, then cross out the things you can't control and deal with things you can.

Remember that the only thing you can control is yourself. Decide that you'll stop obsessing over things out of your control and stick to that decision. Your body and mind will thank you.

....

....

....

....

....

....

....

....

....

....

....

....

....

....

....

....

Deconstruct Your Problems

Give away your problems to the Universe. Write down all your worries and problems. Visualize turning them over to the Universe. Imagine your problems are a balloon, then let it go.

....
....
....
....
....
....
....
....
....
....
....
....
....
....
....
....
....
....
....
....
....
....

Believe and trust now that the Universe will take care of all your problems. Take some time to visualize and imagine now that all is well and your life is exactly as you want it to be. Describe it and write a positive story:

....

....

....

....

....

....

....

....

....

....

....

....

....

....

....

....

....

....

....

Look back on it a couple of weeks or months later, and you will remember that your little problems meant nothing at all - and consequently your current big problems likely mean nothing at all in the big scheme of your life.

Two Cup Manifestation Technique

The two-cup method is another effective manifestation method you can try if you are trying to manifest a specific outcome and turn your situation around.

The working of this method is based on a principle known as dimension-shifting. Think of a period when a big change occurred in your life, and ended altering lots of things about you. Now, that's a dimension shift.

Before proceeding with this technique, it's important to understand what shifting of dimensions really means, and here's the best way to explain it. There are other mini-universes where every alternate situation or scenario in your life happens. These mini-universes are known as dimensions.

So, if you are currently broke and struggling financially, there's another dimension where you are rich or will be rich. And what the two cup manifestation method aims to achieve is to initiate a shift in dimension. That is, moving or crossing from your current situation to another dimension where the outcome you seek is already happening.

Simply put, every positive outcome you desire or the dream and aspiration you want the universe to turn into reality, can become a reality or is currently becoming a reality in another dimension. So, with the two cup manifestation techniques, you will be making a jump from your current dimension where you have the unwanted situation to a new dimension.

How to perform this technique

To perform this manifestation technique you will need

✦ Two cups: one empty and one filled with water

✦ Two labels to identify the cups

✦ A pen

STEP 1

Label the two cups to reflect your current unpleasant situation and the outcome you are trying to manifest. The cup filled with water represents your current situation, while the empty cup represents your desired outcome, and they should be labeled accordingly.

For instance, if you're struggling financially, you could label the water-filled cup "financial troubles," while you label the empty cup "financial abundance."

STEP 2

Sit comfortably in front of the cups and meditate. Concentrate on your current situation and all the struggles you are facing, and also focus on the good feelings you will get from achieving your desired outcome.

STEP 3

Transfer the water. While reflecting on the wonderful feeling of achieving your desired outcome, carefully pour the water into the empty cup.

STEP 4

Be engrossed in the outcome. As you carefully pour the water into the empty cup and while you are still in a meditation mood, focus on the sound of the water as it fills the empty cup. Try to hear, see, and feel it. See yourself stepping out of your current situation and moving into a new dimension.

STEP 5

Meditate on your new outcome. After pouring the water into the empty cup, mediate on the new state of the filled cup and tie it to your situation. Focus on your new reality and immerse yourself in the good feelings that come with your new status.

STEP 6

Drink the water. While in the mood for meditation, drink the water and let your heart be filled with excitement and positivity while doing it. See yourself as now in perfect alignment with the vibrational frequency of the outcome you want manifest.

STEP 7

Discard it. Now, it's time to remove the "desired outcome" label or you can leave it as it is, depending on what your gut feeling says.

STEP 8

Start living in your new reality. Now that you are aligned with your desired outcome, it's time to start living and acting like you have achieved that outcome already, and never let doubt or negativity into your mind.

Read out loud

MY DREAMS ARE MANIFESTING
BEFORE MY EYES.

I NOW RELEASE ANY FEARS OR
LIMITING BELIEFS I MAY HAVE.

I TRUST THE UNIVERSE.

Focus Wheel

The objective of the focus wheel is to help raise your vibrational frequency around anything you want to manifest. It can be something general, such as seeking happiness, or something specific such as manifesting a certain amount of money.

Write your main desire in the center of the wheel, for instance," I am abundant and prosperous." Then populate the rest of the wheel with positive statements and affirmations that support that desire. Examples are "I have my best outfits from the best brands," "I enjoy buying gifts for my friends," "money flows to me in all directions," and so on.

Another example, if your intention is that you want to get fit, you might write, I love providing my body with the respect and nutrition it needs, or I love and appreciate my healthy body. Then every single day, you should take the time to focus on your central intention and take the time to keep yourself focused on your goals as supported by the surrounding affirmations.

When you use the focus wheel this way, you are simply changing the vibrations surrounding your desires, which can create a surge in momentum and make it easier to achieve your manifestation.

Example

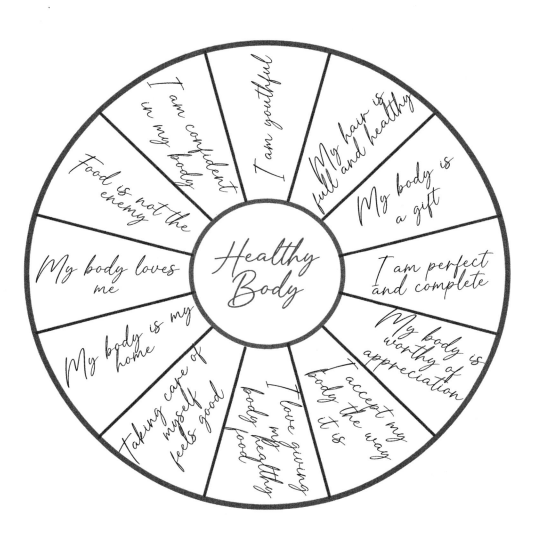

"All of us have within us this amazing capacity to manifest anything that we want into our life."
Steve Harvey

Create Your Own Focus Wheel

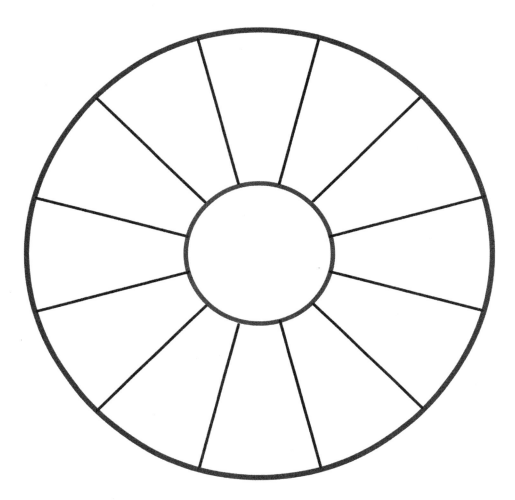

"Thoughts become things. If you see it in your mind, you will hold it in your hand."
Bob Proctor

Create Your Own Focus Wheel

"Once you make a decision, the universe conspires to make it happen."

Ralph Waldo Emerson

Prosperity Game

The prosperity game is a fun game invented by Abraham Hicks. The main objective of this game is to raise your vibration and get you on a pedestal where you are aligned to spend large sums of cash. And in the process, the power of creation within you is awakened. The game requires you to align your emotions as though you were getting real money and spending it in real life. The Prosperity Game expands your creativity and increases your capacity to think about what you desire.

DAY 1

On day one, imagine that the universe has just sent you $1000, and all you have to do is step out and spend that money in your mind. Think about what you'd like to spend the money on, list each thing you will buy with it and the approximation of what it will cost and go ahead and spend it in your mind.

DAY 2

On day two, you only have to imagine yourself receiving double of what the universe sent you the first day, which is now $2,000. And just like the previous day, go and spend it on whatever you want.

DAY 3

Day three is here and it's the day the universe is sending you an imaginary $4,000 and you have to imagine yourself going out to spend it also.

If you are not used to having a lot of money, you will be astonished at how difficult it is to expand your imagination at first. The game is meant to help you change your limiting perceptions of money and get an understanding of what it's like to have a limitless amount of money at your disposal. You can continue for 30 days or as long as you like. By playing the prosperity game you are conditioning your mind to attain new financial heights while also raising your vibration.

DAY 1 - $1,000

....
....
....
....
....
....

DAY 2 - $2,000

....
....
....
....
....
....

DAY 3 - $4,000

....
....
....
....
....
....

3x33
Manifestation Method

3x33 method is also known as the 33x3 or 333 method.

3x33 manifestation method is very similar to the 5x55 technique, the difference is that this manifestation method is faster than the 5x55 method.

STEP 1

The first step to this manifestation method is to set your intention. Decide what you want to manifest. Try to focus on one specific desire for now, so you can clearly communicate to the universe what you would like to manifest. You have to know exactly what you want to manifest and it has to be as specific as possible.

STEP 2

Once you know the one thing you wish to manifest, you want to set a positive affirmation that spells it out as if it has already happened. Don't forget to incorporate the emotional aspect of what you're trying to manifest. Make your affirmation personal and as specific to your desire.

A mindset focused on gratitude is key to achieving happiness. Adding a big dose of gratitude can make your affirmation complete and powerful. Such as:

"I am so happy and grateful now that. . ." or

"I am thankful for. . .".

STEP 3

Once you have found your wish and created your affirmation, you have to write it down 33 times each day for 3 days. It has to be 3 consecutive days..

Although it seems like a very basic task, don't rush through it. Try to stay in the present. You are not just writing down your affirmation. You are attempting to connect your affirmation with your intention and find a deeper sense of meaning and feeling behind the phrases. Hold yourself accountable and be consistent.

When you are done, release the intention. One of the ways to make your Law of Attraction manifestations work a lot faster is to believe you truly deserve what you're asking for.

At the end of the process, don't forget to let go. You should essentially release any mental expectations or attachments to your affirmation and intention. Don't hold any expectations or stress over results.

The key is to hold trust and peace to welcome anything that comes to you. Emotion is the key to manifesting.

You will manifest what you feel.

Follow the 3x33 manifestation method for 3 days and see what magic occurs.

DAY 1
DATE:

MANIFESTATION INTENTION:

1.
2.
3.
4.
5.
6.
7.
8.
9.
10.
11.
12.
13.
14.
15.
16.
17
18.
19.
20.

21. _____

22. _____

23. _____

24. _____

25. _____

26. _____

27. _____

28. _____

29. _____

30. _____

31. _____

32. _____

33. _____

Read out loud

MY SOUL IS READY TO LIVE THE LIFE OF MY DREAMS

DAY 2
DATE:

MANIFESTATION INTENTION:

1.
2.
3.
4.
5.
6.
7.
8.
9.
10.
11.
12.
13.
14.
15.
16.
17
18.
19.
20.

21. _____

22. _____

23. _____

24. _____

25. _____

26. _____

27. _____

28. _____

29. _____

30. _____

31. _____

32. _____

33. _____

Read out loud

I VISUALIZE MY IDEAL LIFE AND I WATCH IT MANIFEST

DAY 3
DATE:

MANIFESTATION INTENTION:

1.
2.
3.
4.
5.
6.
7.
8.
9.
10.
11.
12.
13.
14.
15.
16.
17
18.
19.
20.

21. _____

22. _____

23. _____

24. _____

25. _____

26. _____

27. _____

28. _____

29. _____

30. _____

31. _____

32. _____

33. _____

Read out loud

I AM MANIFESTING MY DREAMS INTO REALITY

ONCE YOU MAKE
A DECISION
The Universe
CONSPIRES TO
MAKE IT HAPPEN

Manifestation Success Story

Use this page to write, illustrate or attach photos, receipts, evidence or proof of your 3x33 Manifestation Success Story. This will help to document your manifesting journey and minimize resistance to future manifestation and the Law of Attraction.

Forgiveness Letter

It's impossible to have relationships without conflicts, and when these happen there's bout to be resentments, anger, and bitterness. There are times when people will say things to you that hurts like a knife, and most of the time, conflicts are something that can have undesired effects on both parties. Both parties can feel badly hurt and hold grudges against each other.

One thing you need to realize, however, is that holding grudges and refusing to forgive someone can be counterproductive because it acts as emotional baggage that holds you down and impedes your progress. It's easy to see grudges as your way of making the other person feel bad. But in the real sense, you are hurting yourself.

Writing them a forgiveness letter sets you free and helps you find that inner peace. Before you write the letter, you want to reflect on everything that happened between you and this person. You want to think of what led to the conflict and also the role you played. Write to them letting them know you have forgiven them. In the letter, you might also want to talk about what you could have done differently. Don't forget the goal of this letter is to set get rid of the emotional baggage holding you back. After writing your letter, you don't have to send it to them. The goal is for you to find inner peace, and you've done the hard work, which is pouring out your emotions into writing.

"It's not an easy journey, to get to a place where you forgive people. But it is such a powerful place, because it frees you."

I Forgive...

....
....
....
....
....
....
....
....
....
....
....
....
....
....
....
....
....
....
....
....
....
....
....
....
....
....
....
....
....
....

Write a letter from your future self

Imagine writing to your future self 5 or 10 years from now. What would you say? What kind of person would you be? What goals would you want to have achieved? Think about what advice you want to give your future self. Doing this exercise can be an extremely insightful experience.

Date ....

....

....

....

....

....

....

....

....

....

....

....

....

....

....

....

....

....

....

Top places I would love to visit

1.

2.

3.

4.

5.

6.

7.

8.

9.

10.

Affirmation Cards

Write your affirmations on these cards. Read them often. You can even cut them out and keep them close to you.

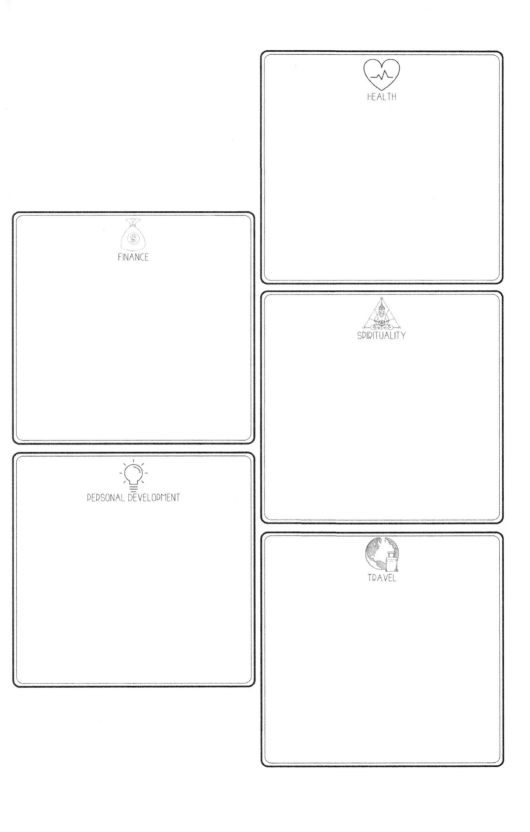

FINANCE

HEALTH

SPIRITUALITY

PERSONAL DEVELOPMENT

TRAVEL

The magic checks from the Universe

The "magic check" method is a powerful and effective manifestation technique where you write a check of what you are trying to manifest, which then prompts the universe to grant your desires. Sounds simple, right? Well, that's just the simplest way to put it.

The main secret to making the magic check method work for you is gratitude.

Express gratitude as though the universe already sent you the money you want. Any time you see or think about the check, be thankful as though you have received and manifested your heart desires.

The checks work because they already are a physical manifestation of the abundance you desire.

"When you think of the things that you want, and you focus on them with all of your intention, the Law of Attraction will give you what you want every time."

Lisa Nichols

Example

Write your name and the value or thing you want to manifest.

The key is to have fun with it, be creative, and use it to make you feel good.

Believe in it: if you order food delivery you have faith that it's going to be delivered to you, and that's exactly what you should do with the checks as well.

Psssst..you can manifest more than just money. You can also manifest experiences or objects. Just write the object's or experience's value on the check.

As an example, if you know you need $5000 to travel to Maldives, you would write $5000 on the check, and you would mention "for my dream trip".

Now that you know what abundance checks are and how to use them, we encourage you to play around with this method and have fun bringing all sorts of abundance into your life.

You can cut them out and keep them close to you or you can put them on your vision board!

The Universal Bank of
Limitless Abundance

LIMITLESS ABUNDANCE · la · MANIFEST YOUR DESIRES

Date _____

Pay _____

To the order of _____

_____

Drawer: The Universe
Account of Limitless Abundance

Signed *The Universe*

This is not an instrument subject to Article 3 of the UCC

The Universal Bank of
Limitless Abundance

LIMITLESS ABUNDANCE · la · MANIFEST YOUR DESIRES

Date _____

Pay _____

To the order of _____

_____

Drawer: The Universe
Account of Limitless Abundance

Signed *The Universe*

This is not an instrument subject to Article 3 of the UCC

The Universal Bank of
Limitless Abundance

LIMITLESS ABUNDANCE · la · MANIFEST YOUR DESIRES

Date _____

Pay _____

To the order of _____

_____

Drawer: The Universe
Account of Limitless Abundance

Signed *The Universe*

This is not an instrument subject to Article 3 of the UCC

Vision Board Cut-Outs

Building a vision board is such an effective way to manifest what you truly desire into your life. Here you will find a range of different quotes, words and affirmations to create a vision board that aligns with your desires and goals.

I AM SUCCESSFUL

I am financially free

I LOVE MONEY, MONEY LOVES ME

My potential to succeed is infinite

I make money easily

I AM A MONEY MAGNET

Success comes naturally to me

Focus on your goal

MOOD CE0,000,000

Vision Board Cut-Outs

I LOVE MY BODY

I am worthy

I AM POWERFUL
AND CONFIDENT

I am comfortable in my own skin

*I am perfect and complete
just the way I am*

My life is full of endless
opportunities for success
and happiness

I AM WHOLE

yes, you can.

Vision Board Cut-Outs

I am ready for love to change my life

I am attracting real connection

POSITIVE MIND
POSITIVE VIBES

And so, she decided to start living the life
she imagined

I ATTRACT HEALTHY AND
LOVING RELATIONSHIPS

MY GOAL IS
financial freedom

DREAM. PLAN. DO.

WHEN YOU FEEL LIKE QUITTING
think about why you started

Vision Board Cut-Outs

MY PEACE IS MY POWER

I release all fear

I am a magnet for positivity, abundance and blessings

I AM IN HARMONY
AND BALANCE

I am free from stress

I VISUALIZE MY DREAM
LIFE AND WATCH AS IT
MANIFESTS INTO REALITY

nothing is impossible

I am healthy, wealthy and happy

Follow your dreams

Notes & Reflections

....
....
....
....
....
....
....
....
....
....
....
....
....
....
....
....
....
....
....
....
....
....
....
....
....
....
....

Notes & Reflections

Notes & Reflections

Notes & Reflections

Notes & Reflections

WHAT YOU IMAGINE YOU CREATE.
TRUST. HAVE FAITH. BELIEVE.
IT'S ALREADY YOURS.

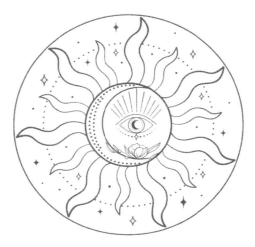

The Universe acts in mysterious ways.

The Law of Attraction is always working.

Trust the process and trust the Universe to bring you the right thing at the right time.

ENVISION THE FUTURE YOU DESIRE.
SEE IT. BELIEVE IT. FEEL IT.

The day you decide that you are worthy of your dreams is the day you will start attracting and manifesting them into your life.

That's all for now!

We would love to hear from you! Your opinion matters to us! Share with us your manifestation success stories and how this journal is helping you - it will create a positive change and inspire others!

We create our journals and planners with love and great care. Yet mistakes can always happen.

For any issues with your journal, such as faulty binding, printing errors, or something else, please do not hesitate to contact us by sending us a DM on Instagram @limitlessabundance_official or email info@limitlessabundanceofficial.com

If you enjoyed this journal, please don't forget to leave a review on Amazon.

Just a simple review helps us a lot!

*We appreciate your love and support,
it means the world to us.*

Instagram
@limitlessabundance_official

info@limitlessabundanceofficial.com

@limitlessabundance

Printed in Great Britain
by Amazon

80304151R00129